When Jesus Came

By the same author—

A Recipe for a Merry Christmas

When Jesus Came

HANDEL H. BROWN

Pastor of the First Presbyterian Church
St. Cloud, Florida

WILLIAM B. EERDMANS PUBLISHING COMPANY
GRAND RAPIDS, MICHIGAN

I dedicate this volume
with devout thankfulness
to my mother
OLIVE HOLDER BROWN
who gives so much
and asks so little
and to my father
CHARLES HENRY BROWN
Student of the Word
Preacher of the Word
Doer of the Word

PREFACE

Last July, Dr. Kenneth L. Wilson, Executive Editor of *The Christian Herald,* asked me to write an article entitled, "What is Christmas made of?" Because of the strict limitations of space, it was not possible to deal adequately with any of the subjects involved. At Dr. Wilson's suggestion, I continued to work on the project until it reached its present size.

I now realize that I am involved in an undertaking that could become interminable, and result in a whole series of books. So I am calling a halt before it gets out of hand altogether.

I wish to thank my admirable Publishers, the Wm. B. Eerdmans Company, for their interest and patience, for the excellent job they do in format and production, for their meticulous handling of detail, and for their insistence upon accuracy.

I wish to thank my lovely wife for her encouragement, for the amazing way in which she puts up with me, and for her help in correcting the proofs.

HANDEL H. BROWN

Feast of Pentecost, 1963

CONTENTS

10 Contents

Part Four

Part Five

Part One

Chapter One

HISTORICAL BACKGROUND

History is not, as someone has said, "just news from a grave-yard." Nor is it necessarily true, as Hegel, the German philosopher, suggested, that history teaches nothing except that man learns nothing from history. The farther backward you can look, the farther forward you are likely to see.

Upon the death of Solomon in 933 B.C., the ninety-two-year-old Kingdom of Israel came to an end. Two separate and independent kingdoms took its place. The Northern Kingdom, which claimed for itself the title of Israel, is better known as Ephraim. The Southern Kingdom was called Judah. The Ten Tribes were in the Northern Kingdom. The Tribe of Judah dominated the Southern Kingdom. The first king of Ephraim was Jeroboam. The first king of Judah was Rehoboam.

In 721 B.C. the Northern Kingdom was conquered by Sargon, king of Assyria. He entered Samaria, the capital city, and carried off Hoshea the king and many of his nobles. Numerous settlers from various parts of Assyria were planted in the country to take the place of the natives who were deported.

The Kingdom of Judah was apprehensive when the Assyrian army invaded the Northern Kingdom. However, Sargon allowed the Jews to maintain a semblance of independence. They paid an annual tribute to their Gentile overlord, but continued to run their own affairs with Hezekiah as their monarch.

The days of Assyria were numbered. The Empire on the Tigris was threatened by the rising of the Second Empire on the Euphrates. In the last ten years of his life, Sargon in Nineveh had to allow a king to reign in Babylon. He managed to extract tribute from him, but he was powerless to depose him.

When Sargon died in 705 B.C., his successor, Sennacherib, made it his first duty to drive Merodach-baladan (Isaiah 39:1) from the throne of Babylon. It was only a temporary respite.

11

Sennacherib was assassinated in 681 B.C. The crime was committed by one of his own sons who was in league with Babylon. Another son, Esarhaddon (2 Kings 19:37), squashed the rebellion. He ruled Assyria from 681 to 669 B.C. He was succeeded by Ashur-banipal (called Asnapper, or "the great and noble Osnapper," Ezra 4:10), one of Assyria's greatest kings. However, treachery, jealousy and intrigue dogged his steps to such an extent that his military expeditions drained the national treasury. Before he died he recognized the signs of Assyria's inevitable collapse.

When Nineveh fell in 612 B.C., the Empire of Assyria came to an end. The Babylonian star had risen for the second time. Pharaoh Necho of Egypt, perhaps remembering stories about the first Babylonian Empire of fourteen hundred years earlier, threw the weight of his forces against the new threat. He was routed at the Battle of Carchemish in 605 B.C. (cf. 2 Chronicles 35:20). The supremacy of Babylon was assured.

The history of Judah now moved rapidly towards its tragic close. The ruling clique began to intrigue with Egypt against Babylonia. In 597 B.C., Nebuchadnezzar moved against the rebellious Jews (2 Kings 24:1). He captured Jerusalem, robbed the Temple and the palace, but evidently did not do much material damage to the city. He deposed King Jehoiakim. He placed Zedekiah on the throne as his vassal. A considerable number of the wealthier and more skilled inhabitants were deported to Babylon.

Unfortunately, Zedekiah was not a strong man. He seemed to have a lot of depth on the surface, but deep down he was shallow. He began well. He appeared to have sufficient sense to realize that Jeremiah was right in advocating obedience to the demands of the conquerors (Jeremiah 37 and 38). But when there was a general movement among the small neighboring subject states against Babylon, he went along with them. Then he turned to Egypt, and entered into an alliance against the oppressor (Ezekiel 17:15).

In 587 B.C., Nebuchadnezzar's army returned. Jerusalem was besieged (2 Kings 25:1ff.). For eighteen months the defenders held out bravely. Famine was the final factor. When the Jews were too weak for further resistance, the invaders breached the walls and entered the city (Jeremiah 39:1ff.).

Jerusalem was destroyed. The Temple, the palace, and all important buildings were systematically burned. The city walls were broken down. The surrounding country was laid waste. Thousands of Jews were massacred. Thousands more were carried away into captivity. The land was left desolate.

From every side the neighboring nations moved into Judean territory. The Ammonites came from the East. The Edomites encroached from the South. The Samaritans swarmed down from the North. It was the end of the first Hebrew Commonwealth.

* * * * *

In 538 B.C., Babylon fell before the might of Cyrus, king of the Medes and Persians (Ezra 1:7, 3:7, 4:3, 5:13, Isaiah 44:28, Daniel 1:21, 6:28, etc.). He had a revolutionary concept of government. It included the unheard-of idea of sending the captive peoples back to their own countries. In the second year of his reign, 537 B.C., he published this proclamation: "All the king-doms of the earth hath the Lord, the God of heaven, given me; and he hath charged me to build him an house in Jerusalem, which is in Judah. Whosoever there is among you of all his people, the Lord his God be with him, and let him go up" (2 Chronicles 36:23).

That same year, forty-two thousand Jews returned to Judea from their exile in Babylonia. Disillusionment followed disaster. Despair followed failure. They returned with high hopes. They were idealists out of touch with reality. They pictured Jerusalem as they had known it as children. They had been removed before it was destroyed. They had refused to believe the reports that had come to them. The painful adjustment to conditions as they really were was prolonged and costly.

Heathen practices adulterated the religion of the land. Pagan social customs, introduced by the large foreign element, were stranger than the things they had found in Babylon.

The Jews who had remained resented their return. The people who had infiltrated from other countries did everything in their power to hinder their resettlement. There were jealousies and factions among themselves. False reports were sent to Cyrus. They made small and slow progress.

The "Second Temple" they built was a very modest affair compared with Solomon's magnificent edifice. They were bitterly disappointed that they had to erect such an unworthy building (Haggai 2:3). Their enemies scoffed at their efforts. They argued among themselves if it was really worth the bother. It was not until 516 B.C.—exactly seventy years after the destruction of Solomon's Temple—that it was completed.

Nehemiah was the last governor of Judea to be sent from the Persian Court. He arrived in Jerusalem in 444 B.C. He was a man of strong personality. He overcame the opposition of those who wished Jerusalem to remain a weak and defenseless city. Its walls were restored. New ramparts were added.

Nehemiah was appalled at the spiritual weakness of the nation. With Ezra, the aged Scribe and Priest (Ezra 7:21), he instituted a series of far-reaching reforms. They were aimed at restoring the purity of both the race and the religion. The Law again became the Constitution of the nation. God was given His rightful place at the heart of Jewish life and affairs.

The importance of this reformation can be measured by the fact that it made possible the survival of Judaism during the struggles of succeeding centuries.

The subsequent history of this tiny State was one of exploitation, defeat and despair. The Jews were pawns in the hands of the great powers. They were held first by one side, and then by another.

Alexander the Great destroyed the Persian Empire in 333 B.C. His domain spread over the world with an unprecedented rapidity. Palestine was included as a matter of course. The young king, however, was most generous in his dealings with the Jews. He granted them self-government. He respected their religious scruples. He excused them from service in his army. The Hebrew people were favorably impressed by their first meeting with the Greeks.

Alexander died at Babylon in 323 B.C. His generals immediately began to quarrel among themselves over the division of the spoils. A long series of wars followed. Palestine was frequently the battleground. Ptolemy seized Egypt. Seleucus made himself king of Syria. Both claimed Palestine. Thus it became a sort of no man's land between them.

Ptolemy won the first round. The land of Israel came under Egyptian control. Jerusalem was captured without resistance. It was the Sabbath when the forces of Ptolemy approached the city. The Jews refused to break the Sabbath law. They would not bear arms even to defend themselves. They went on with their worship as if everything were normal.

It was not until 198 B.C. that the Syrians, under Antiochus the Great, wrested Palestine from the Egyptians. By this time Rome was beginning to assert herself. She had just destroyed the power of Carthage. Her eyes were turned to the East. In an effort to preserve his possessions, the Syrian king agreed to pay a huge tribute to Rome. The only way to raise that kind of money was by intolerable taxation. The subject nations did not fail to kick. Cracks appeared in the structure of the Syrian Empire. The Jews, under the amazing leadership of the fiercely nationalistic Maccabees, entered upon their most glorious era. For sheer heroism and sacrifice, history knows no parallel.

Yet at this stage of its career, the State of Judah was small, poor, depressed and insignificant. It was an indistinguishable part of the Syrian Empire. As a province of Syria, its name was not known along the Mediterranean seaboard. From the time of the Return from Babylon to the rise of the Maccabees, Judea had remained a negligible quantity in the life of the surrounding world.

The Syrian king, Antiochus Epiphanes, tried to stamp out the Jewish religion. He forbade circumcision and the observance of the Sabbath. He ordered all copies of the Law to be burnt. In December, 168 B.C., he personally defiled the Temple by sacrificing a huge swine on the Brazen Altar in honor of Zeus. Portions of the animal were boiled, and the liquid was poured over every part of the Temple.

Antiochus Epiphanes later ordered that such offerings should be made throughout the country. An old priest at Modin refused to perform such a ceremony. When a more "practical" priest stepped forward to obey the edict, Mattathias killed him. Then he and his five sons fled to the hills. They were joined by hosts of the faithful. Guerrilla warfare severely harassed the Syrians. On the death of Mattathias, his third son, Judas, became the leader of the insurgents. Under him, the Syrian armies were defeated and the Jews took Jerusalem. He purified the Temple and reorganized its proper worship under the highpriesthood of his brother Jonathan.

Judas was nicknamed "Maccabaeus," which means "the hammerer." Gradually this became the family name, replacing the more correct title "the Hasmoneans."

Upon the death of Judas in battle, his brother Jonathan succeeded to the leadership. He continued the fight for Jewish independence. He was treacherously slain by a Syrian general. Simon, the last remaining son of Mattathias, was elected leader in his place. He succeeded in negotiating a treaty with the Syrian king, Demetrius II, which guaranteed political freedom to the Jews.

The Maccabean rulers not only raised the small Syrian province into an independent kingdom, but out of Judea they fashioned the Jewish Palestine. It was through these great national heroes alone that the borders of Judea were enlarged, and "Philistia" became "Eretz Israel," with boundaries almost identical to those of David and Solomon.

The five sons of Mattathias were: Simon, Eliezer, Judas, Jonathan and Alexander. Deterioration set in when Alexander's sons, Hyrcanus and Aristobulus, became rivals for the throne.

※　　※　　※　　※　　※

At this point there arrived on the scene a most remarkable man, Antipater the Edomite. He was named after his father, who had been a governor of Idumea. The elder Antipater had seized every opportunity offered by his office to enrich himself. When he became governor, he was hard put to it to make ends meet. When he vacated the position, he was one of the richest men in the land.

His son craved the recognition and esteem that wealth had not brought to his father. Driven by an obsession for advancement, authority and prestige, he exhibited amazing diplomatic skill. There is more than a similarity of titles between him and Doeg the Edomite, who ingratiated himself into the favors of Saul and successfully fed him bad advice for personal advancement. What Doeg was to Saul, Antipater was to Hyrcanus.

Hyrcanus was like putty in his hands. He easily persuaded him that his brother had robbed him of his hereditary rights. They sought help from the Arabs. Aristobulus was soon besieged in Jerusalem. His Sadducean supporters encouraged him to ask the famous Roman General, Gnaeus Pompey, to arbitrate the "family squabble." This was about as sensible as it would have been for the Three Little Pigs to invite the Big Bad Wolf to come inside and help them keep the door closed against their enemies.

Hyrcanus and Aristobulus appeared before Pompey in the city of Damascus in 63 B.C. To their surprise, a third delegation presented itself. This was "The People's Party." It claimed to represent the nation. It begged Pompey to send the contending brothers into exile, and allow the Jewish people to resume their traditional form of self-government under a properly chosen High Priest. As the Sadducees supported Aristobulus, it is thought the People's Party was organized by the Pharisees.

Pompey had no difficulty arriving at a logical conclusion. He had three claimants before him—Aristobulus, Hyrcanus, and the delegation that claimed to represent the nation. He decided in favor of a fourth interested party—Rome.

Judea was incorporated into the Roman Province of Syria. All the extra-Judean territory, which had been gained at such terrible cost, was stripped off, except Idumea. The Greek cities of the seacoast and across the Jordan were set free from the hated Jewish yoke. Samaria and Galilee were also attached to the Province of Syria. Aristobulus was made to march in Pompey's triumphal parade. Hyrcanus became High Priest. Antipater had his power—under Rome.

Although he twice made the mistake of backing a loser, Antipater was able to wriggle out of predicaments that would have been fatal to most men. By the simple expedient of changing sides, he emerged from his defeats stronger than he was before.

After the battle of Pharsalis and the death of Pompey in 48 B.C., a lesser man would have fled to the desert. But not Antipater. True, he had supported Pompey, but Pompey was now out of the picture. So he brazenly went over to the winning party of Julius Caesar. He took not only his tool, Hyrcanus, with him, but also a large contingent of soldiers from Syrian cities and Nabatean strongholds. These troops were just the reinforcements Caesar needed. With their help it did not take him long to bring Egypt to her knees again. In 45 B.C., Caesar appointed him "Procurator," and Hyrcanus "Ethnarch," which means "Chief of the People."

Antipater is important because he was the father of Herod the Great. He had three sons: Phasael, Herod and Joseph. The first two were appointed governors of Jerusalem and of Galilee respectively, when Herod was only twenty-five years of age. At this time he was married to an Idumean named Doris, by whom he had one son, named after his father. He early manifested those gifts for which he is known today. After the assassination of Caesar on the Ides of March, 44 B.C., Cassius, the chief conspirator, betook himself to Syria. He immediately laid the cities of Asia Minor under heavy tribute. The amount demanded of Palestine was out of all reason. Only one area paid its assessment, Galilee. From the beginning, Herod showed that he could be relied upon to fulfill Rome's demands.

Joseph, the youngest of Antipater's sons, does not seem to

have held public office. He was one of Herod's generals and was in charge of the fortress Masada, on the western shore of the Dead Sea. There Herod left his family when the Parthians overran Palestine in 40 B.C. He fled to Rome in search of aid. A double-crossing Parthian general, Pacorus by name, captured and imprisoned Phasael. When he realized the inevitability of his doom, he cheated the executioner by beating out his brains against the wall of his cell.

These were years of rebellion, sedition and sporadic civil wars. Although the Jews hated the Roman rule Pompey had imposed upon them, they seemed to hate one another even more. Tens of thousands of them died in internecine strife. These were the pick of the nation, which was correspondingly enfeebled. The pillage and destruction made the land a wilderness. Josephus sums it up: "Owing to perpetual wars, the Jews were no longer capable of revolting against anyone."

Chapter Two

ECONOMIC CONDITIONS

Even the meanest kind of rebellion costs money. The Jews were in dire straits financially as well as numerically.

They were still essentially an agricultural nation, though not, of course, entirely so. More than forty kinds of crafts were listed by the Rabbis. The trades were handed down from father to son. The son of a dyer was a dyer. The son of a blacksmith was a blacksmith. This had hardened into an almost rigid caste-system.

In the same way, certain cities had become noted for certain products. Just as, today, when you say "Pittsburgh," the automatic association is "steel," so in those days the mention of "Bethsaida" brought the thought of "fish," while that of "Sepphoris" was associated with "weaving." The ancient cottage-industries, such as the manufacture of fine linen and the making of pottery, were quite widespread.

The bulk of the people, however, were not artisans. They were peasant farmers. They owned a small piece of land. They existed on what they could produce from it. The entire family helped with the labor. They grew "subsistence crops" for their own use. If there was anything left over, it was either bartered with one of the neighbors, or taken to the nearest market, where it was sold for money that was used to procure simple necessities.

These "small holders" had absolutely no reserves. Two bad seasons in a row could mean the loss of their property. It could even mean slavery.

On the death of the father, the eldest son normally inherited the farm. The others joined the ranks of the day laborers and the unemployed (cf. Matthew 20:1ff.).

At the other end of the economic scale there was a small class of extremely wealthy landowners. They were the Sadducean aristocracy. Most of them were related to the High Priest, if not by blood, then by marriage (cf. Acts 4:6). A lot

19

of them were absentee landlords. Their estates were managed by "Stewards" (cf. Luke 12:42). Some of them let out the land on a sharecropping basis. Jesus refers to them in His parables (cf. Luke 16:1ff., 21:33ff.).

Commerce had developed to such an extent that on the annual Day of Atonement, the High Priest included a prayer for "a good year of trade"! Merchants had booths in the markets of all sizable towns. There were important and influential Guilds.

Jewish ships, manned by Jewish sailors and laden with Jewish merchandise, sailed the Jordan, the Dead Sea, the Sea of Galilee, the Mediterranean Sea, the Black Sea, the Nile and the Euphrates. These vessels sailed as far as France, Spain, Carthage, and even India. As a result, "international bankers," "shipping magnates," and "merchant princes" became fabulously wealthy. They were despised in Jerusalem as the *nouveaux riches* who paraded their luxury and decadence in mansions of Greek architecture.

"The fulness of the time" was a time full of economic frustration for most of the Chosen People. Palestine possessed a huge class of poor people. Many of them were unemployed. Many were destitute. Many were homeless because their property had been sold for back taxes, or for debt. There was also a small class of inordinately wealthy families—great farmers, merchant princes, bankers, landed proprietors, rich ship owners, and unscrupulous moneylenders who conveniently forgot the injunction, "Thou shalt not lend upon usury to thy brother" (Deuteronomy 23:19), and charged fantastic rates of interest.

The former grew poorer and poorer. They became beggars who roamed the village streets, or brigands who swooped down on the caravans from their mountain dens. The latter grew richer and richer until between the two "there was a great gulf fixed."

      ❈   ❈   ❈   ❈   ❈

Jesus was born into the most heavily taxed nation the world has ever known. The religious taxes alone were more than any modern economy could bear. They were based on the provisions of the Law as interpreted by the Priests, the Scribes and the Pharisees.

The chief tax was the Levites' tenth of all the produce of

the soil (Numbers 18:21,24). This was exacted with scrupulous accuracy (Matthew 23:23). It was for the benefit of the Priests and Levites. Before this "Levites' Tithe" was calculated, two deductions were made. First, the tax of the sevenfold first fruits (Exodus 23:16, 34:22, Deuteronomy 18:4). The first fruits of barley, wheat, grapes, figs, pomegranates, olives, and honey belonged to the Church. Also taken out was one-fiftieth of all the fruit that grew on trees. The remainder was then tithed for the Levites.

That was only the beginning. A *second* tenth was then demanded (Deuteronomy 14:22). This was not for the Priests or Levites. It was placed with the tithe of the cattle, and earmarked for sacrifice. Every three years a *third* tithe was extracted, for the benefit of the poor (Deuteronomy 14:28f.).

Even that was not the end! The firstlings of all animals that might be offered in sacrifice were claimed. A sum of money had to be paid for first-born children, and for the firstlings of unclean animals (Numbers 18:15ff.). This was the "redemption price." The first cake baked with freshly milled flour was taken (Numbers 15:20f.), as well as part of the wool when the sheep were shorn (Deuteronomy 18:4). On top of all this, there was the annual poll tax for the "building fund" of the Temple (Exodus 30:14f.; cf. Matthew 17:24).

You would think that when they had paid their "church dues," the Jews would not have had anything left for the Government. The Greeks, and the Syrians after them, took for themselves *one-third* of the produce of the land and *one-half* of the fruit of the trees.

Herod was a spendthrift. He was always in need of money. He took a proportion of everything grown. We do not know exactly what that proportion was. It can hardly have been as high as his predecessors. There was a bad famine one year, and he voluntarily remitted one-third of the taxes due to him. Herod also collected a tax on everything that was sold in the public markets.

Rome, of course, had to have its cut. Export and import dues were laid on merchandise. There was a Roman water tax, city tax, meat tax, salt tax, road tax, and house tax. These were all on top of the taxes imposed by Herod on these commodities.

Roman taxes were harvested by "tax-gatherers," or "publicans." This was the most hated class in the nation. When Theocritus was asked which was the cruelest of all beasts, he replied that among the beasts of the wilderness, they were the bear and the lion; among the beasts of the city, they were the publican and the parasite.

Publicans had no rights. They were excommunicated by the Jewish Church. They were ostracized by society. They were not allowed to bear witness in a court of law. Their money was not accepted by the synagogue or the Temple. They were lumped together with the other outcasts, "publicans and harlots" (Matthew 21:32). If the shadow of a publican fell on a Pharisee, he was ceremoniously "unclean." Jesus reveals the general attitude of the Jews to the publicans when He bids the Church regard the unrepentant sinner as "an heathen man or a publican" (Matthew 18:17).

The infamous "frontier tax" proved a special hardship. All goods *passing through* a town or state were taxed. Every city gate was a "frontier," and a place of taxing. Pliny tells us that goods were sold in Rome at more than a hundred times their cost in the place where they were manufactured or produced.

Broadly speaking, there was no "middle class" among the Jews. I say "broadly speaking" because, like most generalizations, this has many notable exceptions. We think immediately of the story of the call of James and John. We are told "they left their father Zebedee in the ship with the hired servants" (Mark 1:20). This certainly suggests Zebedee was a man of some means. The fact that he personally engaged in the operation, however, indicates that he was not a wealthy man. Where else can we put him but in the "middle class"? It appears likely that he was one of those rare men of his day who, while born in poverty, was able to rise above it to some extent by his own initiative and industry. Capernaum was large enough to afford him this opportunity.

We think also of the story of Mary, Martha, and their brother Lazarus. The Fourth Evangelist portrays a comfortable home in Bethany. It was a family which was certainly not in need. Its members were on friendly terms with substantial people in Jerusalem (John 11:17ff.). "Six days before the passover," Jesus was the guest of honor at a special supper in this home (John 12:1ff.). The Third Evangelist, however, seems to picture a household where the domestic chores were undertaken by the sisters, without benefit of outside help (Luke 10:38f.). On the whole, they seem to have been "comfortably well off" without being wealthy. They belonged to what we call the "middle class." Probably they were born into wealthy society, and after the death of their parents lived on a decreasing capital.

I say "broadly speaking" also because numerically the middle class was extremely small, so small that relatively it was almost negligible. Geographically, it was limited to Jerusalem and two or three of the largest towns. The vast majority of the inhabitants of Palestine were *'ammê ha-aretz*, the despised proletariat.

The Pharisees loom large in the Gospel story. We get the impression they were everywhere. This is not so. They were almost entirely confined to Jerusalem, where, again relatively, they were not very significant, numbering less than one per cent of the population of the city. They had their representatives in the synagogues of the larger towns. They tried to keep their finger on the pulse of the nation. When John the Baptist began to make quite a stir, they thought it worth their while to investigate. This involved sending delegates from Jerusalem to interview him (John 1:19). The Pharisees made up the greater part of the middle class of the nation.

The only other people who belonged to this small category were minor government officials. We think immediately of Joanna, the wife of Chuza, Herod's steward (Luke 8:3). The Idumean and the Romans were surrounded by career men in the diplomatic, military and administrative services. All of these put together would not be a drop in the bucket of the total population.

The middle class was so small it was not a salient factor in the economy of Palestine at the beginning of the Christian era.

Chapter Three

RELIGIOUS CONDITIONS

Israel was among the nations like a vineyard chosen and cherished (Isaiah 5:7). The Law was theirs to teach them righteousness. The sacrifices were theirs to bring to them a sense of sin. They had the Prophets to warn them. They had the Psalmists to cheer and strengthen them. They had the Covenant to encourage them. And yet, in spite of all, the sap of virtue and godliness had gone out of their soul.

When "the Word became flesh, and dwelt among them" (John 1:14), they did not want what He had to offer. They did not welcome the message He proclaimed. They refused His grace. He offered them sonship in the Kingdom of Heaven. They wanted lordship in the kingdom of this world. He offered them the peace of God. They wanted the kind of peace they could impose by conquest. Because He did not compromise with the popular expectation, their cry of "Hosanna" changed into "Crucify him."

The Third Evangelist tells us they did not recognize the time of their visitation (Luke 19:41ff.). In view of the long preparation for the Advent of Jesus and the widespread anticipation of the Coming of the Messiah, the question arises, *Why* did they fail to know the time of their visitation?

The answer is to be found not only in the confusion of unworthy ideas about the Messiah which were in circulation, but, perhaps even more, in the general uncertainty regarding the nature of religion. Israel was a house divided. It was torn and riven by opposing factions. Each claimed to have the truth, the whole truth, and nothing but the truth.

To even the most casual reader of the gospels, the names of some of the parties are familiar. People who never read the Bible know of the Pharisees and the Sadducees. They may also have heard of the Scribes, the Zealots, the Herodians, and even the Essenes.

The Old Testament knows nothing of the Pharisees and the Sadducees. Yet it is to the Hebrew Scriptures that we must turn for the beginning of these parties.

When Ezra returned from the Babylonian Captivity in 458 B.C., he found the Jews who had remained in Palestine divided among themselves. The question at issue was their relationship to the foreigners in their midst (Ezra 9:1ff.). A Commission was appointed to investigate the situation (Ezra 10:16f.). Unfortunately it was not appointed until after Ezra, by executive fiat, had ordered all Jews who had married alien wives to put them away and resume their national purity (Ezra 10:11). Although the people went along with this harsh ruling in theory (Ezra 10:19), they failed to put it into practice (Nehemiah 6:17ff., 9:2, 10:28f.).

Nehemiah returned in 444 B.C. He had to wage the same war as Ezra. Apparently, he met with as little success (Nehemiah 13:23ff.). The natural leaders of the people, including members of the High Priest's family, were among the chief offenders (Ezra 10:18, Nehemiah 13:28).

As the prosperity of the nation increased, more and more wealth passed into the hands of the priests. A "Temple aristocracy" took the place of those who had been the leaders of the nation before they lost everything when their land was overrun by its enemies.

At the same time, the High Priest, as the only recognized leader of the Jews, gradually assumed whatever political power and authority was allowed to the nation.

It was these two factors, more than anything else, which raised the High Priest and his circle into pre-eminence. In order both to consolidate their strength and to increase their wealth, the members of this élite group were anxious to intermarry with the native aristocracy. They were prepared to sacrifice the sacred uniqueness of Israel for the sake of worldly advantages. They were so brazen about this that they were accused of being apostates.

The patriots who followed the dictates of Ezra and Nehemiah were driven more and more to the other extreme. They began as an exclusive Jewish party. Their exclusiveness increased with time. Their fundamental principle was complete separation from everything non-Jewish. Gradually the application of this principle was widened.

The name under which, in later times, the adherents of the aristocratic party meet us is *Sadducees,* from "Zadok" (1 Kings 1:8). In opposition to them, the *Pharisees* stand for the most uncompromising representatives of the strict, exclusive party.

The meaning of the name *Pharisees* is perfectly clear. Its original Hebrew form *Perusim* can signify only "those who have been set apart," not only from the heathen Gentiles, but also from the great unworthy masses of their own people (John 7:49).

So there developed two opposing religious schools. By constant friction they were brought into ever sharper contrast. The Pharisees were nonpolitical. The Sadducees were the leading politicians. The Pharisees were mostly city dwellers. The Sadducees became the great landowners, and although they maintained magnificent "town houses," they spent most of their time on their country estates. The Pharisees made the whole of life religious. The Sadducees divided life very conveniently into "sacred" and "secular."

The Pharisees regarded the rich aristocracy as "the ungodly" who relied not on God's help, but on their own political astuteness. They accused them of using their vast wealth, and their consequent influence with foreign nations, to the detriment of the Pharisees.

In the heyday of the Hasmonians the Sadducees reached the pinnacle of their power. They aligned themselves with the ruling house. They transformed the earlier Jewish concept of a theocracy into a political doctrine. They secularized the idea of the Kingdom of God for their own benefit.

The Pharisees denounced the Maccabees as usurpers. They looked to God to drop His Kingdom, ready made, upon the earth. It would be ruled by His Vice-regent, the Messiah. He would be of the legitimate royal house of David.

Later, as the fatal struggle with Rome became more and more imminent, the focus of their thought was on the Person of the Messiah. He would be "the son of David," but not "the Son of God."[1] He would overthrow the Gentiles, represented by Rome, and destroy "the wicked," that is, all who did not agree with them! In His Kingdom the power would be in their hands, for it would be the kingdom of the saints, and they were the saints!

[1] This explains Luke 22:70 and John 19:7.

The Pharisees believed in the immortality of the soul, the resurrection of the body, future retribution, and in angels and spirits (Acts 23:6, 8). They also believed in a "limited free will." They gloried in the sovereignty of God. They held to a form of Predestination. Yet at the same time they insisted upon man's freedom of choice, and, therefore, his responsibility. In this particular emphasis, they were the forerunners of the Presbyterians.

On his deathbed, the bloodthirsty High Priest-King, Alexander Jannaeus, instructed his wife Alexandra to give more power to the Pharisees. He probably meant her to pay more attention to spiritual matters than he had done. Alexandra obeyed him literally. She ruled from 75 to 67 B.C. During her reign the Pharisees gained control of all internal affairs, in spite of the fact that they had no policy but "leave it to God, the future is in His hands."

The further subjection of the Sadducees took place under Herod the Great. Under him, they lost almost all their influence, along with most of their wealth. But under the Roman dominion, the High Priest, and with him the Sadducees, regained greater political importance, although they never again played the leading role.

The New Testament provides a great deal of evidence for a composite picture of the Pharisees. They were the strictest Jews (Acts 26:5). They were scrupulous in their observance of the law (Acts 22:3, Philippians 3:5). They were members of the Sanhedrin (Acts 5:34, 23:6). They held to the tradition of the Elders (Matthew 15:2ff., Mark 7:1ff., Luke 11:38f.; cf. Galatians 1:4). They claimed that the whole of tradition was revealed to Moses, who transmitted it orally to Joshua and the Seventy Elders. The difficulty of preserving it intact through so many centuries was evaded by their theory of "Apostolic Succession," which postulated an unbroken line of authoritative teachers. They fasted (Mark 2:8). They tithed (Luke 18:12). They were strict in their observance of the Sabbath (Luke 13:14, 14:1, John 5:16). They performed ceremonial ablutions before meals (Mark 7:3). They refused to eat with "publicans and sinners" (Mark 2:16). They accepted the rule of the Gentiles as God's punishment upon an ungodly nation, but they questioned the legality of paying tribute to Caesar (Luke 20:22).

With the rise of the Pharisees, the external flourished at the expense of the internal. Beneath their numerous ritual exercises there was often concealed an impure, ambitious, haughty disposition, whose aim was to lord it over the crowd.

They bound heavy burdens and laid them on men's shoulders (Matthew 23:4, Luke 11:46). This means they laid great stress on a minute, external, mechanical observance of largely insignificant details. According to this system, the man who fulfilled to the letter all the physical requirements of the law was technically "righteous," quite irrespective of his true character.

It is not surprising that Jesus castigates them as hypocrites who pay tithes, but neglect the weightier matters of the law; men who cleanse the outside of the cup and platter, but within are full of extortion and excess; whited sepulchers, which outwardly appear beautiful, but inwardly are full of dead men's bones (Matthew 23:23ff.).

For the Pharisees, God was Lawgiver and Judge. Religion was not a life of intimate fellowship with God, but a strictly legal walk before God. He was not a Friend trying at all times to help them, but a meanly-disposed policeman who never stopped trying to catch them out.

When they kept the Law, they did so from a wrong motive. Their great emphasis was upon the rewards they were to receive because they were "the people." Their own name for themselves was *Haberim,* which means "brethren." It is a title of superiority indicating that they were members of the true congregation of Israel. They were selfish to the nth degree. Everything they did was not for the sole glory of God. They did it with an eye to what they were going to get out of it at the Judgment Day.

Our Lord's whole teaching regarding God as Father was a criticism of Pharisaic legalism. God *is* Lawgiver and Judge. He is not *primarily* so. First and foremost, He is *Father.* All His activity, and all His relationships, must be evaluated in the light of this stupendous fact. Religion, in essence, is fellowship with "the Father." In this family fellowship there is no place for seeking "rewards." The fellowship is itself the supreme reward.

*   *   *   *   *

Only one of the gospels mentions the *Sadducees* by name. Matthew's account of the ministry of John the Baptist (3:1ff.) contains a reference to the Sadducees which is probably in error. There are three good reasons why it is suspect. First, the Sadducees are associated with the Pharisees. Secondly, from what we know of them, they were hardly likely to be interested in John's message, still less to be influenced by it. In the third place, the parallel accounts in Mark 1:2ff. and Luke 3:2ff., contain no mention of the Sadducees. Matthew's second reference to this group (16:1), also links them with the Pharisees, while the parallel account in Mark 8:11ff. mentions only the Pharisees. In Matthew's other story of those who asked Jesus for a sign (12:38ff.), it was the Pharisees who make the request. The Sadducees were the last people to be interested in signs. Matthew's final references to the Sadducees are in 22:23, 34. The situation calls for them. The Pharisees stay in the background until Jesus has dealt with the Sadducees. This is the only correct reference to the Sadducees by name in the four gospels.

Although the other Evangelists do not use the word "Sadducees," they refer to them indirectly. All these oblique references come towards the end of our Lord's life. They are concerned with the plot against Him. It is generally held that the Sadducees showed no interest in Jesus before His last visit to Jerusalem.

When the High Priest comes into the picture, the Sadducees enter with him. The plot to get rid of Jesus is described in Matthew 26:3f., Mark 14:1f., Luke 22:1f. It was brewed in the home of the High Priest. The Pharisees were in attendance. The Sadducees took the lead. The references to "the court of the high priest," "the chief priests," and "the captains" (of the Temple guard), are to Sadducees. They were the party of the High Priest and the Temple.

They had always been the party of the High Priest and the Temple. Their name indicates that. It comes from *Zadok*, who was a priest in Jerusalem during the reign of David (1 Kings 1:8), and was elevated to the High Priesthood by Solomon (1 Kings 2:35). His descendants held this office down to the Exile.

Ezekiel admits only "the sons of Zadok" to the right of officiating as priests in the new Temple (Ezekiel 40:46, 43:19, 44:15, 48:11). The Sadducees were the priestly nobility.

They refused to acknowledge the authority of the Oral Tradition. They held that only the written law of Moses was binding. Like their northern neighbors the Samaritans, they accepted as Scripture only the first five books of the Bible, which they regarded as the work of Moses.

It seems likely that when the Exiles returned home, these were the only writings officially sacrosanct. The works of the great prophets had not yet won acceptance. It took them a long time to do so. The Sadducees fought against any enlargement of their Scriptures right down the line. What was good enough for Moses was good enough for them!

They were members of the Sanhedrin, and no one questioned their position as Judges. However, they were far more severe than the Pharisees. They clung to the *Lex Talionis.* Where the Pharisees were willing to accept some form of compensation for injury, they insisted upon "life for life, eye for eye, tooth for tooth, hand for hand, foot for foot, burning for burning, wound for wound, stripe for stripe" (Exodus 21:23f.).

They wanted the ostentatious things of life for their own homes. They lived luxuriously. Their liveried servants were equal to those of the Greeks and Romans both in appearance and in ability. But when it came to the Temple, that was a horse of another color. They were not great ritualists. They were not willing to inconvenience themselves for the sake of religion.

They were willing to work with Rome. While they did not collaborate to the extent the Herodians did, they nevertheless were reluctant to miss any chance of raking in the shekels. They sent their sons to Rome to further their education. They considered it quite important that they should know "the right people." They pulled down their old homes and built new ones in the latest Greek style. They were patrons of the arts and the theaters. Their moral standards were not so high as those of the Pharisees. They knew when to turn their heads or close their eyes. "Mr. Worldly Wiseman" would have been a most appropriate name for a successful Sadducee.

The Sadducees were concerned only with this world. They did not believe in a resurrection (Matthew 22:23, Acts 4:1f.). They denied the existence of angels and spirits (Acts 23:8). They did not believe in Providence. They taught that man is absolutely and unconditionally "free."

They were snobs. They looked down their noses at the Pharisees because of their superior wealth. They treated the common people much as the French nobles did in the days of Louis XIV. They despised the patriotic Jews, who wished to resist Rome, as unrealistic hotheads. Because they took no trouble to hide these attitudes, they gradually alienated themselves from the rest of

Jewry and eliminated themselves from Judaism. The Pharisees gained complete control of the religious life of the nation. Their final triumph appears in the *Mishnah*, in which the Sadducees are regarded as heretics.[2]

* * * * *

The entire life of a devout Jew was strictly regulated by the Law. He regarded it as God's greatest gift to Israel. In it he saw the complete revelation of the Divine Will. The Covenant depended upon it. Only in the Law had God made known the perfect Way of Life.

In a nation obsessed with the Law, dominated by the Law, committed to the Law, and held together by the Law, it was inevitable that there would develop a body of men dedicated to its study and interpretation. It is easy to see how they would become the most respected and revered citizens. This group included copyists, editors, students, teachers and commentators. They were called *Scribes*.

Ezra was the Scribe *par excellence* (Ezra 7:6, 10ff., Nehemiah 8:1ff.). His successors were those described by Daniel as "the wise men" (11:33, 12:3). They became the teachers of Israel.

The Synagogue probably originated in the cottage meetings in Babylonia. We know that the "elders of Judah" sought out the prophet in his house (Ezekiel 8:1, 20:1ff.). It is likely they also met in their own homes to discuss their problems, continue their worship, and seek an understanding of God's purpose, as the early Christians did (Colossians 4:15).

The only Old Testament mention of the synagogue occurs in Psalm 74:8. After the Return from the Exile, the synagogue rapidly became an institution in Israel. It was the place where the Law was read and studied. The Jews believed the Kingdom of God would not come until the Law was observed. It was, therefore, most important that it be taught. The Scribes were the teachers.

In the days of the New Testament there were six hundred synagogues in Jerusalem, where the Temple was! There were several in Damascus (Acts 9:2). Every town, village and hamlet in Palestine had its synagogue. Wherever ten Jews settled outside their own land, it was their duty to start a synagogue. There

---

[2] *Mishnah* comes from the Hebrew verb *shanah*, to repeat. In essence it was the interpretation of the written law, collected and codified at the end of the Second Century A.D.

were hundreds and hundreds of them throughout the Roman Empire. Attached to the synagogue was the school. Attendance was compulsory for all boys between the ages of six and sixteen years. The teachers were Scribes.

Like Ezra himself, the Scribes were originally priests and Levites (Ezra 7:12, Nehemiah 8:7, 13; 2 Chronicles 34:13). But pious laymen, particularly of the wealthier classes, began to study the Law for themselves. At first, the priests were the official interpreters of the Law. The laymen acknowledged this. Gradually they formed a relatively independent school of Scribes.

During the Greek period, this independence developed into opposition. It was not antagonism to the priests as such, but to the priestly aristocracy which was willing to become Greek to remain rich. The attempt of Antiochus Epiphanes to wipe out the Jewish religion brought matters to a head. It increased the Scribes' devotion to the Law. It made them more narrow, nationalistic and exclusive. It also greatly enhanced their reputation among the people. They were acclaimed as the leaders of those who were zealous for the Law. They were honored for their willingness to suffer martyrdom for their faith. The forerunners of Patrick Henry, they were respected as "welcoming death with renown rather than life with pollution."

They became Pharisees. They were given seats in the Sanhedrin (Mark 14:43, 15:1, etc.). They gained official stature. They assumed a new character. Beginning as men of sacred letters, they ended as lawgivers and judges.

In the New Testament, the term *Scribe* is used of those learned men who made a special study of the Law. They are called "Lawyers" (Luke 7:30, 11:45ff., 14:3). It is interesting to compare Matthew's account of the question about the Great Commandment with that of Mark. In the former (Matthew 22:35), the questioner is described as a "lawyer." In the latter (Mark 12:28), he is "one of the scribes." The titles were interchangeable. The Scribes are also called "Doctors of the law" (Luke 2:46, 5:17, Acts 5:34). There can be little doubt that the reference to "teachers of the law" (1 Timothy 1:7) reflects the common usuage of another title of the Scribes.

The New Testament distinguishes between "Scribes" and "Pharisees." Yet they are so frequently introduced together that we infer they represented one and the same point of view in theology. It is probably true to say that while all the Scribes were Pharisees, not all the Pharisees were Scribes. In the account of the healing of the palsied man, the Second Evangelist speaks of "Scribes" (Mark 2:6). In the parallel passage in the Third Gospel we have "Scribes and Pharisees" (Luke 5:21). Evidently the terms were synonymous.

The people held the Scribes in great honor. Several passages in the gospels indicate this. The respect accorded to their teaching is shown in the question of the disciples, "Why then say the scribes that Elijah must come first?" (Matthew 17:10, Mark 9:11), and the question Jesus asked in the Temple, "How say the scribes that Christ is the son of David?" (Mark 12:35). They were usually addressed as "Rabbi." This means either "My lord," or "My great one." No wonder Jesus forbade His followers to accept the title! (Matthew 23:8).

The Scribes had no use for Jesus. The feeling was mutual. He accused them of being so concerned with the things of men that they had lost sight of the things of God (Matthew 15:2ff., Mark 7:1ff.).

Although they were supposed to teach the people the meaning of the Law, they were "blind guides" (Matthew 23:16, 24). Instead of being a help to men in their moral and religious life, they were a hindrance (Luke 11:52). Their zeal for making converts was famous everywhere, but it was a zeal without knowledge, and, like all such, it wrought great harm to all whom they influenced (Matthew 23:15).

"And in the hearing of all the people he said unto his disciples, Beware of the scribes, which desire to walk in long robes, and love salutations in the marketplaces, and chief seats in the synagogues, and chief places at feasts; which devour widows' houses, and for a pretence make long prayers: these shall receive greater condemnation" (Luke 20:46f., Mark 12:38., cf. Matthew 23:1ff.).

*　　*　　*　　*　　*

The Scrolls from the Dead Sea, by Edmund Wilson, contains the most readable account of the "Essenes" it has been my good fortune to discover. This is one of the most beautifully written books I have ever read. His easy, delicate style disguises his scholarship. For an introduction to a study of the Essenes it is invaluable. I cannot, however, speak with such unreserved enthusiasm about some of his conclusions.

The discovery of the Dead Sea Scrolls has stimulated interest in this obscure fraternity. Scholars have always known of the existence of this brotherhood. Few people outside the classroom or the study ever heard the name until the Scrolls came to light. Then even newspapers began to write about the Essenes. If, as seems likely, the Scrolls come from them, then we are now in a position to understand them to a greater extent than ever before.

Until now, the verdict of scholars has been "the Essenes are the great enigma of Jewish History." They appeared in the last third of the second century B.C., during the reign of John Hyrcanus. They disappeared with the revolt of Bar Kochba in A.D. 132. In that span of about two hundred and fifty years, they exerted an influence on Jewish history and culture, on the extent and degree of which no two historians seem to agree.

One school of thought sees them as the logical extension of Pharisaism. Another says they were influenced by Oriental modes of thought. While some scholars argue for the purity of their Judaism, others find plentiful traces of such Persian fancies as angelology, demonology, sun-worship, the rejection of animal sacrifices, libations, and distinguishing modes of attire. Were the Essenes Persia's gift to Jewry, or the choicest flower of Hebrew culture?

Their mode of life seems to have been as full of contradictions as the information about them which has survived the ravages of time. Were they a strictly monastic order of men who withdrew to the desert to avoid the lures of the flesh and achieve ascetic holiness? Or did they allow some of their number to live in towns, working as missionaries and recruiting new followers to the fold?

Did they insist that sexual relations were the ultimate in evil, so that one act of intercourse polluted a whole city, or did they permit some of their members to marry so that their Order would be replenished? Did they repudiate social obligations, or did they use their knowledge of herbs and medicines for the common good? Were they primarily concerned with working out their own salvation by washings and fastings, or were they apocalyptists who withdrew from society to await "the day of the Lord," and were their ablutions the means of preparing themselves for that day? Was their primary insistence upon correct doctrine, or were they more concerned with daily life?

About "the great enigma of Jewish history" we wish to know a great deal more than we actually do. Most of our information comes from Josephus.[3] Unfortunately, his statements are not

[3] *Wars*, 2:8:2ff., *Antiquities*, 18:1:5.

objective reporting. They are colored by his purpose and his constituency. He was writing with educated Greeks in mind. He was concerned to show them that there were similarities and points of contact between the Jews and the outside world. Several modern commentators have rejected the trustworthiness of his testimony in no uncertain terms.

We have a certain amount of information about the Essenes which seems to be reliable. They built settlements on the northwest shore of the Dead Sea, in the specific area where the Scrolls were found. Excavators have unearthed what may well be their principal buildings. The main structure has every appearance of being a monastery. They held property in common, even to clothes. An "elected steward" was their business manager. He controlled all their finances. They were charitable to the poor. Some of them worked in the fields between their set times of devotion. Others were employed in the production of articles which could be used for peaceful purposes only. They ate their meals in silence. They ate only specially prepared, simple food. They were so insistent upon this that anyone excommunicated for breaking the rules starved to death, because he refused to eat food which was not prepared in accordance with the dictates of the Essenes.

They adopted unwanted children. They brought them up as if they were their own. They trained them rigorously in their way of life. They dressed them all alike. When they were provided with a suit of clothes, they had to wear it until it was ready to fall to pieces.

They were fatalists in philosophy. They studied magic. They were foretellers of the future. Josephus says one of them ran a school in the Temple on "How to predict the future."

To all orthodox Jews the Name of God was so sacred that to pronounce it carelessly—in some cases to pronounce it at all— was an offense worthy of death. The Essenes went one step further. Their respect for the Law was so great they put the name of Moses on a level with the Divine Name and imposed the same penalty for any irreverent use of it.

They were extremely strict in their interpretation of the Jewish Law. They took the Ten Commandments so literally that they would not even go to the toilet on the Sabbath, for that involved digging a hole in the ground, and what was that but labor? Some of them went even further and refused to get out of bed on the Sabbath, because that involved an unnecessary expenditure of physical energy.

Their one aim was "holiness." They interpreted it in terms of separation. They narrowed it so that it became individualism. They were the ultimate in Pietism. They refused to sacrifice animals because they believed the noblest words of the Old Testament on the subject (Psalm 51:17, 73:1, 1 Samuel 15:22). They sought to offer to God the acceptable sacrifice of a clean heart. Their motive was excellent. Their mechanics were questionable.

They regarded all sensual desires as sinful. They interpreted Leviticus 15:18 as making all sexual relations defiling. They therefore had a low opinion of women. They could find nothing good to say about them.

They were very careful whom they admitted to their Order. Candidates were placed on a rigorous probation for three years. During the first year they were treated as complete outsiders. They were granted no privileges. They were not allowed to eat in the communal dining room. They were strictly segregated. If they proved themselves satisfactory throughout the first year, they were received as novices. For two years they underwent a stringent discipline with few privileges. If they were successful in this trial, they were initiated into the brotherhood with fear-ful oaths no one is known ever to have broken.

Essenism is important because Josephus says it was one of the three main movements in the religious life of the Jews at the time Jesus was born. It may be summed up as a rigid discipline combined with the most thoroughgoing asceticism. They emphasized personal purity more than public worship. For this reason, the Temple was not important to them. They repudiated the official priesthood, but not the idea of priests, for they elected their own. They were the strictest religious order within Judaism. They were the forerunners of the monastics in the Christian Church. Both were outside the main stream of their respective religious movement.

The Essenes are not mentioned in the New Testament. It is possible that John the Baptist was either one of their number, or considerably influenced by them. The latter is the more likely. The Essenes wore simple white tunics, not the kind of garb associated with the Baptist. Their meals were most carefully prepared, and certainly did not consist of "locusts and wild honey" (Matthew 3:4).

Two more "parties" remain to be considered briefly. Neither of them is a religious sect, but that they had considerable influence on religious conditions is hardly to be doubted. "Religion and politics in those days were not separate entities."[4]

There was a party known as the "Herodians" (Matthew 22:16, Mark 3:6, 12:13). They took their name from Herod the Great. Originally, they were his party, his personal adherents, his supporters. They were the group of wealthy, influential and probably young Jews whom Herod found he could trust because they had identified his interests with their own.

After the death of Herod the Great, they attached themselves to his voluptuous son, Herod Antipas, Tetrarch of Galilee (Luke 3:1) and Peraea from 4 B.C. to A.D. 39. Like his Edomite father, he was not a Jew. His mother was a Samaritan woman named Malthace.

The Herodians were Jews. It is not unlikely they were Sadducees. At the beginning of his reign, Herod went on a rampage against the wealthy Sadducees, murdering and pillaging to an alarming degree. It may well be, however, that certain Sadducean families were spared on condition they throw in their lot with Herod.

In Mark 8:15, Jesus "charged them, saying, Take heed, beware of the leaven of the Pharisees, *and of the leaven of Herod.*" But in the parallel passage, Matthew 16:6, we read, "Jesus said unto them, Take heed and beware of the leaven of the Pharisees *and of the Sadducees.*" The impression is that Matthew regarded the Herodians as Sadducees.

We have seen that the Pharisees hated the Sadducees. This might well explain their strange action: "There came certain of the Pharisees, saying unto him, Get thee out, and depart hence: for Herod will kill thee" (Luke 13:31). It was not respect for Jesus, but a desire to pull a fast one on the Sadducees (Herod's party) which motivated their action.

The Herodians were Jews by birth. They were apostates by practice. No ruler was ever more hated by his subjects than Herod. Every loyal Jew, every Jew who was proud to be called a Jew, would joyfully have given his life to rid the land of the "Edomite slave." It is hardly likely, then, that those who fraternized with him were popular with the people, or acceptable to the religious leaders.

---

[4] Joseph Klausner, *Jesus of Nazareth*, p. 279.

The Herodians sought to make the best of two worlds by uniting Judaism with Hellenism. To this end they supported Herod's promotion of Greek customs in Palestine. He built a theater, an amphitheater and a hippodrome in or near Jerusalem for Greek plays and heathen games. No orthodox Jew ever set foot in one of these. But the Herodians had "box seats." They consorted with the actresses. They participated in the games. They gambled on the results.

Instead of making the best of two worlds, the Herodians fell between two stools. They were tolerated by the Gentiles in much the same manner collaborators have always been tolerated by their conquerors. They were despised by their own people as traitors have always been despised by patriots.

❖   ❖   ❖   ❖   ❖

With the exception of the Sadducees, the whole nation of Israel looked forward to the coming of the Messiah. However, the degree of expectation was not the same with all. Neither did they all look for Him to come in the same way. At one extreme there were such pious Jews as Simeon, "waiting for the consolation of Israel" (Luke 2:25), and Anna, looking "for redemption in Jerusalem" (Luke 2:38), who filled their days with prayer and praise. At the other extreme were the *Zealots,* who even tried to hasten the coming of the Righteous One by the indiscriminate use of force.

Although the Zealots were Pharisees in doctrine, they originated in Galilee, which was never a Pharisaic stronghold. Their main strength was always concentrated in the Northern State. Its terrain was well suited to their particular type of guerrilla warfare.

From the time of Pompey they existed in numerous splinter groups which had very little to do with each other. Josephus says they were first organized into a single party by Judas the Galilean and Zadok the Pharisee for the rebellion of A.D. 6-7. Luke tells us of the failure of this revolt (Acts 5:37).

The Zealots were mainly lusty young hotheads who were tired of enduring oppression. They were prepared to go to any lengths to secure freedom and independence. They were the "Home Rule" agitators of the first century. Their outlook was, "We have nothing to lose but our chains." Their battle-cry was,

No tax but the Temple-tax;

No Lawgiver but Moses;
No King but Jehovah.

They fomented many insurrections. Herod never knew what it was to get them off his back. When he wiped out one group, another raised its standard immediately. They were masters of the ambush. They were experts in cloak-and-dagger murders and hit-and-run raids. Their activities were motivated as much by hatred of the oppressor as by love of God.

As is inevitably the case with extreme and uncontrolled fanatics, they soon found it necessary to prove their zeal with a tyranny and violence which matched anything that Herod or Rome ever did. This served only to increase the prevailing confusion. Not only did they add to their professed love of the Law the duty of defending it with the sword, they also arrogated to themselves the right of deciding who among their fellow countrymen were faithful to Moses.

The Zealots were the forerunners of the Mau Mau, and of many underground "resistance movements" of this twentieth century. They were the *sicarii,* so called from the *sica,* or small curved sword they carried under their cloaks. Their policy was the elimination of oppression and opposition by assassination. When Paul was arrested at the Temple in Jerusalem, he was accused of being the Egyptian insurrectionist who had enlisted the aid of the Zealots (Acts 21:38).

Josephus was violently opposed to this movement. What he says about them, therefore, is to be taken with a grain of salt. The Zealots were not respectable enough for him. He did not want his sophisticated readers to think they were typical Jews. So he tried to dissociate them from the main stream of the national life. To distinguish them from the Pharisees, Sadducees and Essenes, Josephus describes the Zealots as "the Fourth Philosophy" of the Jews.[5] The "Fourth Philosophy" was the philosophy of violence.

Josephus has many unkind things to say about them. He freely labels them "adulterers," "murderers," "fanatics," "brigands" and "robbers." Yet even he has not only to admit, but also to admire both their steadfastness and their tremendous courage. "A certain aged Galilean, one of the fanatics, had seven sons, and when they would have obeyed Herod's command and left their cave, he stood at the mouth of the cave and killed them all

[5] *Antiquities,* 18:1:6.

one by one; and when Herod held out his hand and promised not to punish him, the old man only reviled the king for his Edomite origin and threw himself over the precipice."[6]

Victory or death. They knew no middle course. Compromise was unthinkable. Inactivity was cowardice. Failure to harass the enemy in every possible way and on every conceivable occasion was treachery.

There was a Zealot among the Twelve. In the first and second gospels he is called "Simon the Canaanite" (Matthew 10:4, Mark 3:18), to distinguish him from Simon Peter. However, "Canaanite" is incorrect. It should be "Canaanean." This does not designate the place of his birth, but the political action group to which he belongs. The New English Bible is correct in translating it, "Simon, a member of the Zealot party." In the two treatises of Luke, he is called "Simon Zelotes" and "Simon the Zealot" (Luke 6:15, Acts 1:13).

It is an amazing thing that this disciple of violence, this apostle of hate, should remain faithful to the non-violent, ethical concept of the Kingdom taught by Jesus, while Judas Iscariot was the one who betrayed Him in the hope of turning Him into a Zealot.

---

[6] *Antiquities,* 14:15:4f., *Wars,* 1:16:4.

Chapter Four

"A DECREE FROM CAESAR AUGUSTUS"

The first Roman Emperor was born in the Eternal City on September 23, 63 B.C. He was named Gaius Octavius, after his father, who had added luster to the honorable family name by becoming its first Senator. He died, however, before his son was five years old. The following year, his mother married L. Marcius Philippus who, while his stepfather in name, proved to be a worthy father to him.

His mother, Atia, was the daughter of Julia, sister of Julius Caesar. When Caesar was murdered in the Senate House, on the Ides of March, 44 B.C., Octavius learned that he had been designated his heir. He was eighteen years old at the time. He was studying at Apollonia in Illyria, where he had been sent by his illustrious uncle. He immediately added the names "Julius Caesar" to his own.

His mother pleaded with him not to pursue his claims. She pointed out that more of Caesar's friends than enemies had been in the band of assassins. She stressed Octavius' youth and inexperience. She warned him of all the pitfalls in Roman politics. He listened to her dutifully and patiently, and thanked her for the advice. Then he set out to get what was legally his.

To the amazement of the seasoned politicians and to the despair of his rivals, in an incredibly short time he had firmly established himself not only as the leader of a powerful segment of the Senate, but also as the darling of the people. Within months he was well on the way to becoming the master of Rome.

In November, 43 B.C., Octavius, Anthony and Lepidus were formally appointed to supervise the reorganization of the Commonwealth. They were known as "The Second Triumvirate." Lepidus was soon seen to be the weakest member of the trio and easily squeezed out of real power. Then began the struggle for supremacy between Anthony and Octavius.

However, in 40 B.C., they effected a reconciliation. Anthony married Octavius' sister, Octavia, and the two brothers-in-law divided the Commonwealth between them. Anthony accepted the eastern part, and Octavius the west. Caesar spent the following years in the monotonous task of consolidating his position. Anthony succumbed to the charms of Cleopatra, the sex maniac who was on the throne of Egypt. She had lived openly in Rome as Julius Caesar's mistress. When he was murdered, she returned hurriedly to her own land. Rome was disgusted with Anthony's conduct, and the fact that Cleopatra bore him three children did not help matters.

When the news reached Octavius that Anthony was about to divorce his sister in order to marry the sultry Egyptian beauty, he was tempted to undertake a military expedition against him immediately. However, documents fell into his hands revealing the joint plans of Anthony and Cleopatra to establish an independent Eastern Empire which would eventually overthrow Rome. War was declared against Cleopatra only. Octavius moved swiftly and remorselessly.

His forces defeated those of Anthony and Cleopatra at the Battle of Actium, on September 2, 31 B.C. He pressed the campaign. On August 1, 30 B.C., he captured the strategically vital Egyptian city of Alexandria. Anthony and Cleopatra immediately committed suicide. With her death, the dynasty of the Ptolemies came to an inglorious end.

A tremendous triumphal parade awaited Octavius on his return to Rome. He was tumultuously hailed as the Savior of the Republic and the Restorer of Peace. On January 11, 29 B.C., the doors of the Temple of Janus, the god of war, were closed for the first time in two hundred years.

On January 16, 27 B.C., the Senate named him *Augustus*. That title had never before been conferred upon a living person. It had a sacred association. It had been reserved for religious shrines and groves which were thought to be possessed with divine power. His full name was Gaius Julius Caesar Octavius Augustus. He was known as Augustus. The Greek form is *Sebastos*. The word means "reverend," "venerable."

❋   ❋   ❋   ❋   ❋

Augustus was one of the world's great men. He was not an "intriguer." He was not a "politician." He was a consummate master of statecraft. He conceived and carried out a scheme of political reconstruction which kept the Empire together, secured peace and tranquillity, encouraged trade, increased culture, and preserved civilization for more than two centuries.

He restored the Republic. The various branches of government resumed their proper functions. The Triumvirate was abolished. Augustus reserved controlling authority to himself because, while he tried to respect the Senate, he found it impossible to respect many of the Senators. It was his desire to be a "Constitutional Ruler."

After two early and unsuccessful marriages had ended in divorce, he married Livia Drusilla, wife of Tiberias Claudius Nero. She was a woman of great perception. For the fifty-two years of their marriage, she proved to be a wise counselor and loyal ally. During this time, no domestic scandal was ever associated with his name. Augustus was known as "a stern and moral man."

He recognized that solid family life is the indispensable foundation of a truly great nation. He introduced many important laws seeking to stabilize family life on a worthy level. He was the first Gentile ruler to see that "families that worship together stay together." He never ceased to encourage the corporate family veneration of the gods.

His personal ability was tremendous. His capacity for hard work was prodigious. Tacitus tells us he had an eye and a mind for detail which were unparalleled in the ancient world. He was methodical in everything he did. He personally checked and rechecked every report he received. All new information had to be examined in the light of what he already knew.

Wherever he went, he carried with him a little book in which he entered everything—the number of soldiers in the army, the number of divisions in the field, the taxes received from different countries, how much they were in default, the names of men whose ability suggested promotion, the amount of tribute which could be expected from conquered countries, disaster areas which needed help, means of improving trade, the taxes which could be levied on commerce, and the like. Augustus was constantly alert.

Early in his career he was brilliantly successful in numerous military ventures. Later on, he showed a flare for sending the right generals to the places of unusual difficulty. He knew when to order them to advance and when they had to be content to hold the line. He succeeded in ending civil war once for all. His grateful subjects hailed him as the "Restorer of the Common-wealth and Champion of Freedom." He drove the pirates out of the Mediterranean. He secured the borders and outposts of the Empire. He subdued the Germans between the Rhine and the Elbe. He dreamed of a Roman Germany reaching to the North Sea.

Yet Augustus is not to be evaluated solely on his military accomplishments, fantastic as they were. To him, they were merely the basis for greater and more humanitarian feats. He was prouder of the *Pax Romana* which he gave the world, than of all his martial victories put together. He was grateful for those periods in which the emphasis on strife was least.

His youth had been spent in arduous study under the watchful eye of his able and ambitious mother and stepfather. This bore fruit in later years. He gave the Eternal City its first Public Library and furnished it with the literary masterpieces of the ancient world. He placed a sound emphasis on education. Culture became not a fad but a condition during his reign. He was the patron of Vergil, Ovid, Livy, and Horace. Men of letters were more important to him than men of muscle. He gave his name to a significant age of literature.

Augustus thought deeply on many subjects. He was always active in the field of law. He was capable of arguing cogently with the best lawyers and judges. In religion, he familiarized himself with the lore of his race and with the multitudinous religions of his varied subjects.

His hobby was architecture. He threw himself into an ambitious building program with great enthusiasm. He was not content to know the theory of architecture. He had to know the fundamentals of construction as well. He saw no reason why strength should be divorced from grace. He combined them in an expanse of beauty equalled only by the glory that was Greece.

About the time of the birth of Jesus, Augustus turned his attention to currency. There was no unifying system of exchange, or principle of coinage. Each country made its own money. The situation was chaotic. Augustus instituted far-reaching currency reforms. He saw the need for standardization throughout the Empire. The coins he minted were distributed throughout the world in as fair a manner as possible. The old tokens were called in. The Jews hated receiving anything which bore the image of a man, but, as the new currency was alone acceptable as payment of government taxes, they had very little choice.

As a class, historians have failed to do justice to the genius which was Augustus. He is remembered today only because it was in his reign that Jesus was born. Yet it is probably true that only two men in modern times have equalled him in the diversity and intensity of their interests, Robert Browning, the English Poet, and Theodore Roosevelt, the American President.

The wise master-statesman had ordained that every fourteen years an estimate should be made of the population and resources of the Empire—in the proud Roman phrase, "The whole world" (Luke 2:1).

His scepter swayed the movements of the world's affairs. It ordered the tread of humble footsteps on the road from Nazareth to Bethlehem. It filled that sleepy city with an unfamiliar stir.

But the swing of the Imperial Scepter, and the movements of many feet on distant roads, were one with the measure of a song that was born in heaven and breathed in men's wondering ears by the Spirit of the Living God.

As we look back, we see the Emperor on the high throne of world power. In the same glance we see in far Syria two humble townsfolk of Nazareth, whom his word had bidden on an untimely journey to Judea.

When Augustus died on August 19, A.D. 14, at Nola, a few miles from Rome, in the same room in which his father had died before him and on the anniversary of his entrance upon his first consulship fifty-seven years before, he did not know that in Galilee there was a carpenter's apprentice in His teens, whose followers would spread out to the ends of the earth, and proclaim His infinite glory for centuries after the Empire of the Caesars had crumbled into dust.

Chapter Five

"IN THE DAYS OF HEROD THE KING"

The Edomites were the descendants of Esau (Genesis 25:30). They were as much the "children of Abraham" as the Jews. Yet between the progeny of Esau and that of Jacob there was nothing but bad blood. This was contrary to the specific ordinance of the written Law (Deuteronomy 23:7).

The Jews never forgot the promise made to Rebekah during her pregnancy, "Two nations are in thy womb, and two manner of people shall be separated from thy bowels: and the one people shall be stronger than the other people; and the elder shall serve the younger" (Genesis 25:23).

When John Hyrcanus, son of Simon Maccabaeus, conquered the Edomites in 109 B.C., and compelled them to adopt the Jewish religion, that ancient prophecy was thought to be fulfilled. However, in 55 B.C., the year in which he invaded England, Julius Caesar appointed Antipater the Edomite as the Procurator of Judea.

Everyone important in that turbulent era seems to have been involved, in one way or another, in the fabulous career of the son of Antipater, Herod the Great—even the Roman renegade, Anthony, and the Egyptian sexpot, Cleopatra!

Mark Anthony got him proclaimed King of Judea by the Roman Senate in 39 B.C. Herod was then in his thirty-seventh year. For the next thirty-four years he controlled the destiny of the Jewish people. He was one of the most versatile, colorful and brilliant figures of the eminent Augustan epoch.

As soon as he was proclaimed king, Herod hurried to his realm. He found Jerusalem armed to the teeth to keep him out. He laid siege to the city. After several months, he realized his army was inadequate. He withdrew to Samaria. While waiting for reinforcements he diverted himself by marrying Mariamne, the beautiful and proud descendant of the Hasmonean royal house. Somehow he found time to drive the Parthians out of the country. His brother, Joseph, was killed in battle near Jericho during this campaign. The war against the Parthians lasted until the close of 38 B.C.

In the spring of 37 B.C., Herod again set out for Jerusalem. This time he was supported by Sosius, with eleven Roman legions and six thousand cavalry. It still took him six months to subdue the Hasmonean loyalists.

When the walls of the city were finally breached, the infuriated Roman soldiers went berserk. They would not listen to orders. A dreadful massacre ensued. In an orgy of destruction the mercenaries killed men, women and children without rhyme or reason. Herod waded through the blood of the innocent to ascend his throne.

The Jews reckoned Herod's reign, not from 39 B.C., when he was made king of the Jews, but from 37 B.C., when he seized control of Jerusalem and established himself in power.

Herod began his rule in the usual Oriental fashion. If the Roman troops had wantonly shed the blood of the common people, Herod just as furiously butchered the wealthy. Yet this was not due to caprice. He was as shrewd as he was ruthless. He executed not only all his former enemies, but also all his potential rivals. Included in this massacre was the majority of the wealthy and influential members of the Sadducean Sanhedrin. This did more than destroy the active resistance to him. The confiscation of their property also enriched his coffers.

To please his Hasmonean mother-in-law, Alexandra, who had the ear of Cleopatra, Herod appointed his seventeen-year-old brother-in-law, Aristobulus, to the high-priesthood. When he was presented to the people at the Feast of Tabernacles, he received such a tumultuous welcome that Herod's jealousy was aroused. Upon secret orders from the king, the unfortunate youth was drowned at Jericho. Herod's fervent protestations of sorrow at this terrible "accident" and the lavish funeral he arranged for the deceased, did not deceive Alexandra, and she became his enemy for life. He seems to have persuaded his wife of his innocence, at any rate for a time.

The victory of Augustus and the death of Anthony confronted Herod with a serious danger. Ever loyal to his personal friends, he had done all he could for Anthony, in spite of Cleopatra's liaison with his foes. He now felt that Augustus would be justified in looking upon him as an enemy.

Herod, like his father under similar circumstances, dashed off to meet the new ruler of the world. Removing his royal insignia, he appeared before the Emperor and, without denying his friendship for Anthony and his regret at Anthony's death, frankly offered Augustus the same friendship and loyalty which he had given the defeated traitor.

This attitude appealed to Caesar. He probably saw in Herod a realist in politics. He judged him to be one who could be trusted to serve Rome, and Rome's master, faithfully.

Augustus accepted Herod's offer of friendship. He confirmed him as King of Judea. As if that were not enough, he increased Herod's jurisdiction by adding to his kingdom some lands on the eastern side of the Jordan and a number of pagan cities along the Mediterranean coast.

Herod was thoroughly detested by his subjects. He was hated as a tool of Rome. He was loathed as the one responsible for the fall of the popular royal house. He was despised as an Edomite. He was feared for his private army of secret police. Yet he proved to be Israel's greatest king. He was able to preserve his state from every tyranny but his own.

For nearly forty years he governed the kingdom so efficiently that territory after territory was given him by Rome. Jerusalem once again became the nominal capital of the State. Its walls were rebuilt. It was granted an outlet to the sea by the return of the port city of Joppa.

Under the government of Herod, Judea became the greatest of all the eastern kingdoms allied with Rome. He vastly increased its wealth. He ruthlessly exterminated the brigands, making the roads safe for life and property. He obtained many concessions favoring the Jews. In particular, he won for them exemption from military service and permission to pray *for* the Emperor instead of *to* him, thus safeguarding the purity of their worship and their faith.

Yet Herod made no secret of the fact that he preferred the Greeks to the Jews. He confessed that he did not love the people over whom he ruled and into whose religion he had been circumcised. He could not forget that his fiercely independent parents and grandparents had been forcibly "converted." Neither could he help that condescending sneer which said, plainer than words, "You Jews thought you had mastered us Edomites. Well, look at me! In less than two generations, you have an Edomite ruler, and there's nothing you can do about it."

We cannot be surprised, therefore, that all the material and legal benefits which Herod conferred upon the Jews were received coldly, without gratitude, and often resentfully.

✹ ✹ ✹ ✹ ✹

Herod embarked on a building program for which there was no precedent in the entire history of the Hebrew people. He restored the city of Samaria, long in ruins, and named it *Sebaste* in honor of the Emperor (27 B.C.). He wanted a protected port which would be the base of communications with the western world. The most convenient place he could find was Strato's Tower, about thirty miles south of Mount Carmel. To shelter the vessels from the violent southwest winds which blew along the coast, a breakwater had to be constructed. In an engineering feat almost as great as the building of the pyramids, an enormous mole nearly half a mile long was completed in a short time. This supported a pier which was two hundred feet wide. It was defended by a wall and towers. It was surrounded by broad landing wharves. It enclosed a harbor as large as that at Athens. A huge fleet could ride at anchor in perfect safety. Above the harbor rose the city. Herod named it "Caesarea" in honor of his friend on the imperial throne. It eventually became the leading city of Palestine. Years later, when Roman Procurators had succeeded to Herod's power, Caesarea was their official residence and capital. It was there that Vespasian was proclaimed Emperor in A.D. 69. Under Alexander Severus, it became the metropolis of Syria.

Herod was determined to do for Jerusalem what Augustus had done for Rome—transform it from a city of mud into a dazzling creation of marble.

He completely rebuilt the Temple. He doubled the size of its courtyard. Its grounds were a mile in circumference. It was constructed of white marble, overlaid with gold and jewels. It gleamed high on the summit of Zion. It was a spectacular sight to pilgrims as they toiled over the brow of Olivet on the Jericho road. One awe-struck visitor wrote to Rome of "the great gold and pale marble Temple hanging against the peacock sky of Jerusalem." It gave rise to the widespread proverb, "Whoever has not seen the Temple of Herod has seen nothing beautiful."

Herod surrounded the elegant sanctuary area he developed with beautifully fashioned walls, some of which rose to a height of seventy-five feet. His cornerstones were terrific. One has been excavated measuring sixteen feet long and thirteen feet wide. He was thorough in his planning. The vast courtyards contained cisterns, irrigation, and a drainage system adequate for removing offal and debris.

A strange mixture of arrogance and consideration, Herod was so careful to guard against offending the religious scruples of the Jews that he had selected priests taught the trades of mason and carpenter, in order that no unconsecrated foot should defile holy ground. Herod himself appears never to have entered the shrine which he made possible at the cost of millions of dollars.

It took only eighteen months to build the actual Temple. Eight years more were required to finish the surrounding courts and porticoes. The last detail was not complete (cf. John 2:20) until the time of Albinus, less than ten years before it was reduced to ashes by the conqueror's torch.

Herod's overriding ambition was to found a dynasty. He wanted to make his kingdom world-renowned for culture and progress. He took as his model the legendary figure of that other King of the Jews, Solomon.

It is interesting to compare Herod and Solomon. They were alike in many ways. Both were men of exceptional ability. Both were voluptuaries. Both made the Temple in Jerusalem a wonder of the world. Both had strong sympathy with foreign ideas. Both cherished great schemes for the aggrandizement of the nation. Both discovered that these plans were opposed by popular sentiment as being contrary to the true destiny of Israel. Both turned to foreign powers for assistance, Solomon to Tyre, and Herod to Rome. Both achieved a greatness which did not outlast them by a single generation.

Like Solomon, Herod placed too high a burden on the economy of the country and thereby hastened its end. Not only did he bedeck his own land with magnificent buildings, amphitheaters, and gymnasia, but even Tyre and Sidon, Greece and Asia Minor, Rhodes and Antioch, Athens and Pergamon. Money was required for all this.

Although a vast influx of wealth made Palestine richer than at any other time in its entire history, there was no pretense of anything approaching equality of distribution. It benefited only the few who were in a position to take advantage of it.

But Herod's taxes were levied on all. They became unendurable. The same thing had happened in the days of Solomon, so that when he died the representatives of the people came to his successor, Rehoboam, with the petition, "Thy father made our yoke grievous: now therefore ease thou somewhat the grievous servitude of thy father, and his heavy yoke that he put upon us" (2 Chronicles 10:4). Immediately after the death of Herod, the people demanded of his son, Archelaus, that he "lighten the annual taxes and abolish the duties that were exacted mercilessly on everything bought and sold in the markets."

Herod's ambition to found a dynasty was never realized. He was king by the will of Caesar, for his lifetime only. He was not allowed to establish a hereditary ruling family.

Yet he became one of the most famous men of his day. In the land he ruled, he was despised. Throughout the Greek-speaking cities of the Empire, his name was uttered with respect and awe. His own people spat in the dust when they referred to him as "the Edomite slave." The rhetoricians who enjoyed his benefits in the great cultural centers of the ancient world were loud in their praises of "Herod the Great."

*   *   *   *   *

Domestically, Herod failed to distinguish between trifles and treasures. His final years were embittered by sordid intrigues within the palace itself. The image of him which has come down to us is that of a monster satiated with the blood of his own family. Like the King of Nemi, he walked his groves of jealous wrath with a drawn sword, waiting for the destroyer of his realm.

There is probably no royal house in any land or age in which bloody feuds raged in an equal degree between parents and children, husbands and wives, brothers and sisters.

Joseph, the husband of Herod's sister Salome, was accused of intimacy with Mariamne. Although there was no truth in the charge, Joseph was executed. Alexandra was thrown into prison as the cause of the mischief.

Five years later, in 29 B.C., Mariamne was executed for allegedly bribing a servant to poison her husband. But Herod loved her with wild passion. To divert his thoughts, he gave himself up to excesses. Her death almost brought him to complete insanity. He refused to believe she was dead. He would order his servants to call for her. His days and nights were passed in frantic agony. One by one, he destroyed the minions who had carried out the decree of the servile court.

When hope of his recovery had been abandoned, something happened to engage his activities. He learned that Alexandra was plotting to secure the throne for herself and for Mariamne's sons. This news roused Herod. He ordered Alexandra's immediate execution (28 B.C.). All who were suspected of complicity in the conspiracy suffered the same fate.

Herod had ten wives. Included among them were two of his nieces, and the daughter of the High Priest, Simon bar Boethus. But he never succeeded in shaking off his remorse at the death of Mariamne. Years later, he added three stately towers to the magnificent new walls of Jerusalem. He named the first after his friend Hippias, the second after his favorite brother, Phasael. The third, which was by far the most costly and ornamental, was the monument of Mariamne.

From the hour of her death he trusted no one. The torture chamber, the secret police, and the executioner's sword were his chief allies. He lived in a nightmare of suspicion and fear. One after another he destroyed, not only his numerous succession of wives, but also most of his own children.

His eldest son, named Antipater after the father he loved and admired, accused Mariamne's two sons, Alexander and Aristobulus, of conspiring against the throne. Herod appealed to Rome. With the Emperor's permission, they were tried at Berytus. Herod himself appeared in Court and testified vehemently against them. They were condemned to death and removed to Samaria, where they were strangled (7 B.C.). This blemished Herod's name across the world.

Once his rivals were out of the way, Antipater regarded his succession as assured. However, Herod did not trust him sufficiently to allow him any freedom. When he was told his father was dying, Antipater bribed his guards to free him. They immediately reported this to the king. Herod's pain was so intolerable he was preparing to commit suicide when the messenger interrupted him. The news revived him somewhat. Only five days before he expired, he ordered the instant execution of Antipater and had his body thrown into a nameless grave.

By this time he was known far and wide as a merciless tyrant. The Emperor Augustus, who acknowledged himself to be his friend, said of him, "It would be better to be his *sow* than his *son*."

> On that hard, Pagan world, disgust
> And secret loathing fell,
> Deep weariness and sated lust
> Made human life a Hell.
>
> —Matthew Arnold

When Herod lay dying of a painful, loathsome and incurable disease, he commanded his sister Salome that the chief men of the nation should be assembled in the circus he had built at Jericho, and murdered *en masse* at the hour of his decease, so that their kindred at least should have some cause to weep for his death. Happily, the order was not obeyed.

This was the Herod who butchered the little ones of Bethlehem because of a rumor that among them there might be one to threaten his tottering throne.

Matthew portrays the aged king in his cunning and cruelty as a desperate man alarmed by the coming of a new King who was seemingly weak, but actually Divine. This is the clash which shakes the history of mankind. Herod had magnificence. Christ was born in a manger. Herod had boundless energy. Christ was a helpless Babe. Herod had power, and used it to cruel ends. Christ had compassion, and a different kind of power. Herod was crafty. Christ was guileless. Herod had "all Jerusalem with him." The Outcast in the stable seemed to be almost unbefriended.

The riddle of history is this: How does goodness survive when badness has both cunning and the sword?

The answer lies in a governance of history above and beyond the wit of wicked men. Matthew traces that governance. The Gentiles from afar worship Jesus. Herod in the center of Jewry seeks to kill Him. But his will is not God's will. His way is not God's way. His time is not God's time. Outwardly, everything was on his side. There was no apparent possibility that the Babe could escape his wrath. Yet escape it He did. It was the Lord's doing. There is no other explanation.

Jewish writers have always declared that the reign of Herod was their midnight hour. Be that as it may, it gave us the Bright and Morning Star. It was then that the Light of the world appeared to illuminate the dark Hebrew sky with the auroras of a new and fadeless dawn.

Chapter Six

THE DATE OF OUR LORD'S BIRTH

When someone asks us "the date," it is not too difficult for us to reply. We give the month, the day, and the year. We don't add "A.D." We take it for granted that it is "the year of our Lord," that it is so many years since the birth of Jesus.

For centuries, however, Christians knew no such reckoning. For more than five hundred years after Jesus had lived and died, the old calendar was used. It began not with the birth of Jesus, but with the founding of Rome.

About the middle of the sixth century of our era, Dionysius Exiguus, the abbot of a monastery at Rome, proposed in his famous *Cyclus Paschalis* that a Christian calendar should be adopted, dating everything from the birth of Jesus. The proposal met with immediate and universal acceptance. It is certain, however, that in calculating the beginning of the Christian era, Dionysius made a mistake of several years.

The first gospel informs us that Jesus was born before the death of Herod the Great (Matthew 2:1ff.). We know from secular records, coins, histories and inscriptions that his decease occurred in 4 B.C. Matthew does not indicate how long before the death of Herod Jesus was born. The sketchy account of the Flight into Egypt suggests only a brief sojourn there, but gives no exact information as to its duration.

When we turn to Luke's account, we find he speaks in sweeping rather than detailed terms. An edict *(dogma)* had been issued by Caesar Augustus "that all the world should be enrolled. This was the first enrollment made when Quirinius was governor of Syria." Everyone obeyed the injunction (Luke 2:1ff.).

Luke is concerned only with the immediate relationship of the edict to the birth of the Saviour at Bethlehem. It was the occasion that brought Mary and Joseph to Bethlehem. He does not even tell us how the census was carried out in Judea; whether

by Herod and his officers in obedience to Imperial fiat, by the
governor of some adjoining province who was ordered to relieve
Herod of the responsibility, or by a special representative of the
Emperor sent from Rome for the job.

Luke was a Gentile. A Jew would have known that Quirinius
was never *governor* of Syria under Herod the Great. He served
in that capacity from A.D. 6 to A.D. 9, during which time he conducted the "second" census to which Luke refers in Acts 5:37.

Tertullian states that the census at the time of our Lord's birth
was conducted by Saturninus, not Quirinius, but that contradicts
the date he gives elsewhere for the birth of Jesus (3 B.C.), because Saturninus, who succeeded Marcus Titius as Governor in
9 B.C., was himself succeeded by Varus in 6 B.C. Varus continued
in office until after the death of Herod the Great.

It may well be, however, that Quirinius was sent to Judea to
conduct the earlier enrollment. Rome did not always trust even
its best local representatives. Herod had just received a severe
letter from the Emperor in which Augustus said, "I have hitherto
treated you as a friend, but now I shall treat you as a subject." It
took Herod quite a time to clear himself of the complaints which
had been made against him by the Arabian Syllaeus and to climb
back into the Emperor's good graces. It is quite in keeping with
the character of Augustus that in the meantime he showed his
displeasure by sending a subordinate Roman official to conduct
Rome's business in Herod's territory.

If it is objected that Varus, not Herod, would have been responsible for the enrollment, it can be pointed out that the Jews
never took kindly to any census. It was ingrained in them that
it was contrary to their religion (cf. 1 Chronicles 21:1; cf. 2
Samuel 24:1). The taking of a census was always a risky business
(Acts 5:37). Quirinius was a man who had shown himself very
capable in military affairs. Varus had no military reputation. He
may well have continued to administer the internal affairs of the
province, while Quirinius was sent as the special representative
of the Emperor for a special task. Examples of this are fairly
common in Roman history.

It should be remembered that Justin Martyr states that Quirinius was *Procurator* at the time of the census. This gives weight to
the suggestion that although Varus was *Governor* of Syria under
Herod at this particular time, yet Quirinius may have held some
office in virtue of which he undertook the census. When we

further consider that the Greek word for *Governor* was used to translate several Latin titles for which there was no exact Greek equivalent, the matter should not cause any anxiety. In any case, Luke is not merely giving a date. He is implying that Quirinius was in some way connected with the enrollment, and this is entirely feasible.

Some scholars have ascribed great importance to the statements of Justin Martyr, Tertullian and Chrysostom, that in the public archives at Rome there was a register of the enrollment under Augustus, which proved beyond doubt that Jesus was born at that time. Some people even claim that Tertullian gives the exact words as he found them, *Maria ex qua nascitur Christus.* How credulous can you get? Our Lord was not commonly known as "The Christ" during His lifetime. It is ridiculous to suggest that this title was entered on His "birth certificate."

There is only one definite date given in the gospels and, unfortunately, it is not much help. The Third Evangelist says, "In the fifteenth year of the reign of Tiberius Caesar, Pontius Pilate being governor of Judea ... the word of God came unto John the son of Zacharias in the wilderness. And he came into all the country about Jordan, preaching the baptism of repentance for the remission of sins" (Luke 3:1ff.).

Tiberius became Emperor in A.D. 14, on the death of Augustus. The "fifteenth year" of his reign would bring us to A.D. 29 for the beginning of the public ministry of John the Baptist. How long he had been preaching when Jesus came to be baptized, we do not know, but if He was then "about thirty years of age" (Luke 3:23), He must have been born about 1 B.C., or *three years after the death of Herod the Great.*

Most chronologists date the Baptism of Jesus in A.D. 26. If He was then thirty years of age, the date of His birth would be 5 B.C.

When Jesus celebrated the Passover at Jerusalem at the beginning of His ministry, He was told, "Forty and six years has this Temple been a building" (John 2:20). Herod began the restoration of the Temple "in the eighteenth year of his reign." According to Jewish reckoning, he ascended the throne when he entered Jerusalem in 37 B.C., which would make "the eighteenth year of his reign" 20 B.C. Add to this the "forty and six years," and we again get A.D. 26, indicating that Jesus, who was then about thirty years old, was born in the year 5 B.C.

If we inquire as to which month Jesus was born, we must admit that the gospels give us only two small hints.

We are told that Zacharias was "of the course of Abia" (Luke 1:5). This was the eighth of the twenty-four classes of priests who officiated at the Temple for one week at a time, in turn.

When Herod's magnificent Temple was destroyed by Titus, August 5, A.D. 70, the first class had just entered on its service. If we work backwards to 6 B.C., we find that the course of Abia was on duty April 17 through 23, and October 3 through 9 of that year.

The question then is, on which of these two occasions did Zacharias officiate in the Holy Place? We do not know. If the announcement were made to him during the former, then the birth of John the Baptist may be placed near the beginning of 5 B.C., and that of Jesus six months later (Luke 1:26, 36). If the angel Gabriel appeared to him during the second period, then John was born in the middle of 5 B.C., and Jesus towards the end.

The second hint is contained in the words, "There were in the same country shepherds abiding in the field, keeping watch over their flock by night" (Luke 2:8). There is no reason, so far as climate is concerned, why the shepherds could not have been in the fields in the middle of winter. The climate in Judea is mild. On other grounds, *it is more probable* that they would be near Bethlehem in December than in mid-summer. There is repeated evidence among Jewish writers that the flocks were taken to the distant summer pastures in March, and brought home again in November.

Although the birth of the Son of Mary is the supreme event of history, it is difficult, perhaps impossible, to determine its precise date. When Luke speaks of Mary's sudden visit to Elisabeth, he dates it, "In those days" (Luke 1:39). Again, when he mentions the Imperial Decree, it was "In those days" (Luke 2:1). Perhaps he was deliberately vague.

At any rate we know this, that while heaven is careful to give us the purpose, the promise, and the fulfillment, the Divine Spirit does not care to reveal to us the exact moment when the promise became a realization. "When the fulness of the time was come, God sent forth his Son" (Galatians 4:4).

Chapter Seven

THE SOURCES OF THE CHRISTMAS STORY

The book of the Revelation has always been a happy hunting ground for expositors and commentators. I do not know how many different explanations of the "four beasts full of eyes behind and before" (Revelation 4:6ff.) have been offered to the curious. The devout fancy of the early Christian Fathers regarded them as emblems of the four Evangelists. According to St. Augustine, the Lion is the symbol of Matthew, the Man of Mark, the Calf of Luke, and the Flying Eagle of John.

The Lion and the Calf are the only two Evangelists who mention the birth of Jesus. Indeed, they are the only writers in the New Testament who refer to this great event. It is from them, and from them alone, that we derive what are called "The Birth and Infancy Narratives."

The Gospel according to Matthew was written by a Jew for Jews. It was produced under the shadow of an overwhelming catastrophe. Jerusalem had not merely "fallen" to the Romans, it had been systematically and totally destroyed by them. Some of the most terrible words our Lord ever uttered found literal fulfillment: "They shall not leave in thee one stone upon another" (Luke 19:44).

During the hideous days of the siege, thousands of the inhabitants starved to death. Thousands more were slain by roving bands of looters. Cannibalism was practiced. All who tried to go over to the Romans, in a vain attempt to save their lives, were crucified around the city until there was neither wood for crosses nor room left to plant them.

The few survivors were led captive to Rome. There they were forced to march in the triumphal parade of Titus. He exhibited the golden candlestick, the table of shewbread and the silver trumpets of the Temple as part of his spoils.

When Jerusalem fell to Titus, he ordered that only the three towers built by Herod the Great be spared. Everything else in the city was so completely demolished that for the next sixty years there is no record of anyone living there.

> *The nymphs are gone, the fairies flown,*
> *The ancient gods for ever fled;*
> *The stars are silent overhead;*
> *The music of the spheres is still,*
> *The night is dark, the wind is chill,*
> *The later gods have followed Pan*
> *And Man is left alone with Man.*
> —Israel Zangwill

It is against this background that we must place the writing of Matthew's gospel. Here was a Jew preaching to Jews whose existence as a national entity had come to a sudden end and whose religious life had gone up in smoke with the Temple. Matthew, the hopeful Jew, had a message for the hopeless Jews of his day.

*   *   *   *   *

There has been so much emphasis upon "Matthew the Jew" that we are sometimes in danger of forgetting "Matthew the Christian." He was a Christian writing for Christians. He presents the Gospel as it was understood in the primitive Christian churches of Palestine. They were predominantly, and in many cases exclusively, Jewish.

Matthew seeks to show his disillusioned compatriots that Jesus was the Messiah. As such, He was the fulfillment of all the ardent hopes and aspirations of the prophets, the psalmists and the seers. So his constant refrain is, "That it might be fulfilled which was spoken by the Lord through the prophet" (1:22, 2:15, 2:23, 4:14, 8:17, 12:17, 13:35, 21:4, 26:54, 26:56, 27:9), to which is coupled the phrase "Thus it was written by the prophet" (2:5, 11:10, 26:24, 26:31).

Luke, on the other hand, was a Greek. He wrote for the Greeks. He is an outstanding representative of the first Gentile Christians whom Paul gathered into churches outside Palestine, principally in the great seaports and metropolitan areas at the eastern end of the Mediterranean Sea. Luke wrote "The Gospel of the Greeks."

This does not mean Matthew proclaimed one Gospel and

Luke another. They both preached the same Gospel. You have only to read carefully the two Advent stories to discover agreement in fundamentals.

Their accounts are in accord not only as to the central fact of the Virgin Birth, but also as to the manner of it. They both insist it was a supernatural event due to the operation of the Holy Spirit.

Agreement is also found on the following five other points which are of considerable importance:

    (1) At the time of the Annunciation, the Virgin Mary was engaged to Joseph (Matthew 1:18, Luke 1:27).

    (2) Neither Mary nor Joseph chose the Name of the Child. They were instructed to call Him "Jesus" (Matthew 1:21, Luke 1:31).

    (3) Jesus was born in Bethlehem of Judea (Matthew 2:1, Luke 2:4ff.).

    (4) Jesus was born in the reign of Herod (Matthew 2:1, Luke 1:5).

    (5) Jesus was brought up at Nazareth (Matthew 2:23, Luke 2:39, 51).

      *   *   *   *   *

Matthew and Luke possessed a great deal of information which was common to both of them. However, they approached it differently. It may well be that each of them uncovered some facts which the other did not. But basically they had one and the same Gospel. They emphasized different aspects of it. Their personal approach to whatever information they had was conditioned by three things: their heredity, their education, and the readers they had in mind.

Matthew stressed those elements in the new Faith which would appeal to Jews. Luke brought to the fore the things which would appeal to the Gentiles, most of whom were ignorant of Jewish ideas. However, as we shall see, this does not mean that either *excluded* the items which were stressed by the other.

When Matthew compiled his genealogy, his aim was to present Jesus *the Jew*. So he naturally began with the statement that He was "the son of David, the son of Abraham" (1:1).

Luke was concerned to show His relevance for mankind. So he traced the lineage of Jesus to the beginning and showed Him to be "the son of Adam, who was the son of God" (3:38).

Matthew, the Jew, was anxious to present Jesus as the Messiah for whom Jewry longed. That is why he began with such a detailed genealogy. He set out to prove that Jesus was the rightful Messiah according to Jewish law. He traced His descent from Abraham (1:1), from David and the kings of Judah (1:6ff.), and from (Zerubbabel 1:12f.), who was the head of the Jewish community after its return from Exile (Haggai 2:23, Zechariah 3:8, 4:6ff.). All this showed that Jesus had the necessary racial qualifications to be the nation's Deliverer.

Luke, the Gentile, was writing for Gentiles who were familiar with Greek ideas of universalism. He presented Jesus in His common brotherhood to man, and His native Sonship to God.

The genealogy of Matthew incorporates Jesus with Israel. The genealogy of Luke unites Him with mankind.

Matthew saw Jesus as the final product of Judaism. Luke saw Him as the originator of a new humanity. Matthew interpreted Jesus in terms of the Old Testament. Luke presented the Jesus with whom we are familiar through the writings of his friend Paul.

Matthew saw Him as a Redeemer descended from Abraham and as a King who belonged to the Royal House of David. Luke saw Him as descended from Adam. For Luke, as for Paul, He was the Second Adam, the Creator and Head of a new and universal race.

Matthew never forgot the Kingship of the Messiah. He was "born King of the Jews" (Matthew 2:2). Luke never forgot that He was a Universal Saviour. The Good News was "to all people" (Luke 2:10). He came to be "a light to lighten the Gentiles" (Luke 2:32). He was "the Dayspring from on high," risen "to give light to them that sit in darkness, and in the shadow of death" (Luke 1:78f.).

* * * * *

It has long been suggested that Luke obtained his special nativity information from Mary the Mother of Jesus. There is, of course, absolutely no outside proof of this. Yet it is an attractive and, I believe, a reasonable hypothesis.

The story is told in such a fresh and delicate manner that it is extremely difficult to think Luke received it in the form of stereotyped tradition. It is not soiled by much handling. It is not cut and dried by repetition.

Further, it reflects a woman's point of view. The coloring is feminine. The atmosphere is sensitive. There is an indescribable grace and a quiet loveliness enveloping the whole episode.

Luke himself insists that he traced all things accurately from
the beginning (Luke 1:1ff.). He spared no effort in ferreting out
new sources of information. It is not unreasonable to suppose
that he consulted living witnesses as well as written documents.
One such witness may well have been the Virgin Mary. The fact
that she was long dead when the book first saw the light is no
argument against this suggestion. Indeed, it could be used in
favor of it. A doctor does not usually divulge the confidences of
his patients during their lifetime. Luke, as Paul's personal physician (Colossians 4:14; cf. 2 Corinthians 12:7, Galatians 4:13ff.),
accompanied him to Jerusalem (Acts 21:17). The manner in
which he describes that experience suggests he was no stranger
to the Holy City.

If Luke's story is from the point of view of Mary, Matthew's
is from the standpoint of Joseph. He, rather than Mary, occupies
the center of the stage.

Matthew emphasizes Mary's betrothal to *Joseph* (1:18), the
perplexity of *Joseph* (1:19), the announcement to *Joseph* (1:20),
the appearances to *Joseph* (1:20, 2:13, 19, 22).

But, as has been suggested already, while the Evangelists em-
phasized different points of view, they did not do so exclusively.
Mary is as prominent in Matthew's account as Joseph is in
Luke's.

As we read their records, we find that it is the Jew, Matthew,
who brings the Gentiles from the East to sit with Abraham,
Isaac and Jacob in the Kingdom of God (Matthew 8:11, 2:1).

It is the Gentile, Luke, who portrays the fidelity of Mary and
Joseph to Jewish customs (Luke 2:22ff., 2:41). It is he, not
Matthew, who describes the Temple scenes. He shows us the
crowd "praying without at the time of incense" (Luke 1:10). He
knows how long the service is supposed to last (Luke 1:21).
He places the altar in its correct position (Luke 1:11). He informs us that the Jewish priest Zacharias lived "in the hill
country of Judea" (Luke 1:39).

It is the Gentile, Luke, not the Jew, Matthew, who shows us
the devout representatives of the Faith of Moses, Simeon and
Anna, praising God for the fulfillment of His promise to the
Chosen People.

Jew and Gentile paint the picture of the birth of Him in whom
"there is neither Jew nor Greek," but "all are one" (Galatians
3:28).

Part Two

Chapter Eight

ZACHARIAS AND ELISABETH

Josephus tells us there were more than twenty thousand priests living in Judea "in the days of Herod the king." We may doubt his accuracy, but we cannot escape the conclusion that there must have been an awful lot of priests for him to be able to make such an assertion.

The general character of the priesthood was deeply tainted with the materialism of the times. Many of them were like those whom Malachi denounced as degrading the Temple services of his day (2:1ff.). They were blind leaders of the blind.

Not a few, however, were truly religious men. We are told that after the Resurrection of Jesus "a great company of the priests were obedient to the faith" (Acts 6:7).

There are good people in the worst times. When Elijah thundered against the house of Ahab, he complained that all the people had forsaken God to worship Baal. His moving declaration, "I, even I only, am left; and they seek my life, to take it away" (1 Kings 19:14) was answered by God's reassuring word, "I have left me seven thousand in Israel, all the knees which have not bowed unto Baal" (1 Kings 19:18).

At the time Jesus was born, darkness covered the earth, and gross darkness the people. Yet there were saints scattered abroad in every part of the land. The faithful kept bright the light of true religion. God had not left Himself without witnesses.

Among them were Zacharias and Elisabeth. He was a priest (Luke 1:5). He had been so careful to observe the law regarding the marriage of priests (Leviticus 21:7ff.) that he had married the devout daughter of a priest. She was a descendant of Aaron. She was named Elisabeth after the wife of Aaron (Luke 1:5, Exodus 6:23).

She was as godly as himself. They were not unequally yoked together. The record says they were "*both* righteous before God, walking in all the commandments and ordinances of the Lord

63

blameless" (Luke 1:6). She brought to her marriage with a priest much that she had learned in watching her mother as she attended to her daily chores in a priest's house. She had long ago discovered that one priest in a house is sufficient. She was content to follow her own duties. She did not try to instruct her husband how to perform his. She learned to read his mind, anticipate his wishes, and so think his thoughts that without her his work would have been less worthy. Together, they made a wonderful team.

Their home was an example of domestic harmony. Their personal lives were beyond reproach. Everything they did brought glory to their Creator. Yet they were childless (Luke 1:7).

This condition was regarded as a disgrace among Orientals generally (Genesis 30:23). The Jews regarded it as punishment for sin (Leviticus 20:20f., 2 Samuel 6:23, Jeremiah 22:30).

Zacharias and Elisabeth had prayed long and earnestly for a child. Their request had not been granted. They had reached the age when they had to reconcile themselves to the fact that they could no longer reasonably expect their wishes to be fulfilled.

* * * * *

When David was king, he divided the priests into twenty-four groups. They were to officiate at the Temple in turn for a period of one week (1 Chronicles 24:10, 2 Chronicles 8:14). Abijah, a descendant of Eleaser the third son of Aaron and his successor as High Priest (Numbers 3:32), gave his name to the eighth class of priests. Zacharias belonged "to the course of Abijah" (Luke 1:5).

However, of these twenty-four groups, only four, those of Jedaiah, Immer, Pashur and Harim, returned from the Exile (Ezra 2:36ff.). These four were subdivided into six each, and the resulting twenty-four classes were given all the old names. So Zacharias did not belong to the original course of Abijah, for that perished in the Captivity.

When the time came for the band of Abijah to serve in the Temple, they solemnly cast lots to see who should have the high honor of entering the Holy Place. The lot fell on Zacharias (Luke 1:9).

The presence of "the multitude" (Luke 1:10) suggests the day was either the Sabbath, or a great national feast day.

After the lamb had been slain, and before it was offered in sacrifice, the President gave a signal; and Zacharias, barefooted and robed in white, passed up the steps, accompanied by the two assistants he had chosen.

One of them carried the Golden Censer. It contained half a pound of sweet-smelling incense. The other carried a bronze censer in which were live coals taken from the Brazen Altar. Slowly and reverently they passed into the Holy Place. It was the only time in their entire ministry that such an honor would be theirs.

The attendants removed the ashes from the altar. They spread the fresh coals in their place. The incense was emptied into the hands of Zacharias. Then they prostrated themselves and withdrew. They were careful to retreat backwards, so they would not turn their backs upon the double curtains (the "veil") separating the Holy Place from the Holy of Holies, into which no man was allowed to enter save the High Priest, and he only once a year, on the Day of Atonement (Hebrews 9:7).

Zacharias was alone in the dim light of the seven-branched candlestick. The worshipers waited outside, hardly daring to breathe. At the cry of "Incense!" from the President, he spread the fragrant gum upon the coals. Then and there, heaven broke the silence of four hundred years.

        ❋   ❋   ❋   ❋   ❋

As Zacharias was performing this ritual, suddenly there stood in front of him, where no mortal man should be, an angel of the Lord (Luke 1:11). He was on "the right side of the altar." This would place him between the altar and the golden candlestick. On the left side of the altar was the Table with the Shewbread (Exodus 40:22). The angel identified himself as Gabriel (Luke 1:19).

In the whole of Scripture we are given the names of two heavenly beings only, "Gabriel" (Daniel 8:16, 9:21, Luke 1:19, 26) and "Michael" (Daniel 10:13, 21, 12:1, Jude 9, Revelation 12:7). The word *Gabriel* means "Man of God." *Michael* means "Who is like God." In the Bible, Gabriel is the angel of Mercy and Michael is the angel of Judgment. It is interesting that in other Hebrew literature their roles are reversed.

In the presence of the supernatural, Zacharias "feared and trembled" (Luke 1:12). The angel used the lovely phrase which was to become almost the theme song of the gospels, "Fear not." Then he informed Zacharias that his prayer was heard.

What prayer?

From what we know of Zacharias, from the kind of man we feel he must have been, it is inconceivable that, on that solemn and unique occasion when he stood in the Holy Place as the representative of the whole nation, he should have uttered selfish prayers on behalf of his wife and himself. He was a nobler man than that.

Further, the pathetic words, "I am an old man, and my wife is well stricken in years" (Luke 1:18) indicate a reluctant hopelessness antedating this experience. Years before, he had given up hope of ever having a son of his own.

We must suppose he was conscientiously fulfilling his task, the task to which he was consecrated, the task which reached its glorious consummation on this memorable day when he was privileged to enter the Holy Place, the task of praying for Israel. He had been brought up to believe that a prayer in which there was no mention of the Kingdom of God was no prayer. It is natural to suppose he was praying for the good estate of the Chosen People. He conceived their highest well-being to be the establishment of the Kingdom of God. Zacharias was praying for the coming of God's Kingdom to Israel.

In the midst of his fervent intercession, it was unexpectedly revealed to him that God's Kingdom was at hand: "Thy prayer is heard" (Luke 1:13).

The angelic declaration is followed by the conjunction "and," in the sense of "also," "in addition to that." If his prayer were for a child, we should expect the conjunction to be "for," so that it would read, "Thy prayer is heard, for thy wife Elisabeth shall bear thee a son." But the message comes, "Thy prayer is heard. The Kingdom of God is at hand. Also thy wife, Elisabeth, shall bear thee a son." Like Solomon (1 Kings 3:11ff.), Zacharias received the higher blessing for which he prayed and also the lower blessing for which he did not ask at this time. Such, at any rate, is a possible interpretation of the record.

There is, of course, another possibility. It may be that when the angel said, "Thy prayer is heard," he was not referring to the specific prayer of that great day at all, but to the constant and fervent prayer of many years. He may have meant, "The prayer which you and your devout wife have been bringing to the Throne of Grace for many years has not fallen on deaf ears. Now is the time of its fulfillment."

One thing is certain—when Zacharias returned home that day, he knew he was to become a father.

We often mistake the strength of our desire for the strength of our faith. The desire of Zacharias was strong enough. Yet his faith faltered (Luke 1:18).

When the early Christians prayed for the release of Peter from the jail of Herod Agrippa, God granted their request "while they were yet speaking." When they were told their prayers were answered, they would not believe the messenger. Indeed, they told her she was mad (Acts 12:14f.).

Zacharias had believed in God all his life without the benefit of signs. When the angel appeared, he was sceptical. Like Abraham (Genesis 15:8), he asked for a sign (Luke 1:18).

Of him to whom much is given, much is required in the way of faith. The unbelief of Zacharias was rebuked. "Thou shalt be dumb until the day that these things come to pass" (Luke 1:20). Daniel also was dumb after a similar experience (Daniel 10:15f.).

The offering of incense was symbolic of prayer (Revelation 5:8, Malachi 1:11). The people worshipping in the courts of the Temple were praying while the sweet-smelling smoke was rising from the altar within. The President chanted the age-old prayer, "May the God of mercy enter the sanctuary, and be pleased to accept the sacrifice of His people." The response of the congregation was, "Blessed be the name of the glory of the Kingdom of God for ever."

When the priest re-entered the courtyard from the Holy Place, he dismissed the people with the traditional Benediction, "The Lord bless thee and keep thee; the Lord make his face shine upon thee, and be gracious unto thee; the Lord lift up his countenance upon thee, and give thee peace" (Numbers 6:24ff.).

On this occasion, the people grew restive waiting for Zacharias. It was not merely that they wanted his blessing so that they could go home. It was contrary to all precedent for a priest to prolong his stay in the Holy Place. They did not know what kept him (Luke 1:21).

When he finally appeared before them, he was unable to pronounce the Benediction. He stood before them as silent as a sepulcher. He had to dismiss them with signs. They went away understanding that "he had seen a vision" (Luke 1:22).

❖   ❖   ❖   ❖   ❖

Zacharias returned to his wife in the Judean hills. The name of the city is not mentioned. There is an old Jewish legend which says John the Baptist was born in his father's house in the city of

Hebron. For a long time this was popular belief. However, it is not widely accepted today. There is another ancient tradition which designates a small village about four miles west of Jerusalem as the home of Zacharias and Elisabeth. It is now called by the natives *Ain Karim*.

"Ain Karim is a flourishing village, situated on the left bank of Wady Beit Hanina. In the midst of it, on a kind of platform, stands the Franciscan convent of St. John in the desert. The church is large and handsome, and includes the site of the house of Zacharias, where St. John Baptist was born. It is a kind of grotto, like all the other holy places, and is profusely ornamented with marble, bas-reliefs and paintings. In the center of the pavement is a slab with the inscription *Hic Praecursor Domini natus est*. About a mile distant is the place known to the Latins by the name of the *Visitation*. It is situated on the slope of a hill, where Zacharias had a country house. Tradition says the Virgin Mary, on her visit, first went to Elisabeth's village residence; but, not finding her there, proceeded to that in the country, where accordingly took place the interview related in Luke 1:39-55. The spot is marked by the ruins of a chapel, said to have been built by Helena. About one mile farther is the grotto of St. John, containing a little fountain, beside which the place is shown where he was accustomed to rest."[1]

The New Testament is silent about all this. It merely informs us that Zacharias "departed unto his house" (Luke 1:23).

In due time, John the Baptist was born there. On the occasion of his circumcision, the speech of his father was restored. "Zacharias was filled with the Holy Ghost," and sang the glorious *Benedictus* (Luke 1:67ff.).

At this point, Zacharias fades from the scene. We have no definite knowledge of his end. Several of the early Fathers, including Origen, identify him with the Zacharias who is mentioned in Matthew 23:35. They further allege that this brutal murder was the work of Herod. If that be so, then Herod the Great murdered Zacharias, and Herod Antipas, son of Herod the Great, murdered John the Baptist, son of Zacharias (Matthew 14:1ff.).

---

[1] Porter, *Handbook for Syria and Palestine*, I, 235.

Chapter Nine

JOHN THE BAPTIST

"When John the Baptist appeared, not the oldest man in Palestine could remember to have spoken even in his earliest childhood with any man who had seen a prophet.... In these circumstances it was an occurrence of the first magnitude, more important far than war or revolution, when a new prophet actually appeared."[1]

We must expect, therefore, startling facts to accompany such an exceptional event. Luke presents those facts.

The angel Gabriel appeared to Zacharias. He informed him of the impending birth of a son to Elisabeth and himself. Both of them were past the normal age of parenthood. At a word from his strange visitor, Zacharias became dumb. Everything connected with the incident (Luke 1:8-23) was supernatural.

Perhaps the most interesting part of the story is that in which the heavenly visitor describes the coming child. The John of our imagination is wild, rugged, fearless, and austere. In the eyes of God's messenger he is more attractive. His very name is winsome. "John" (Luke 1:13) means either "The Lord is gracious," or "The Gift of God." For his wonderful parents, it would mean both. John was not only "a gift," he was also "gifted."

After a silence of four hundred years, God was again visiting His people. The saying, "Many shall rejoice at his birth" (Luke 1:14), proved to be true. His birth was the awakening of new hopes. It was the dawn of a new day.

The Scribes and Pharisees did not accept John's baptism (Luke 7:30, Matthew 21:27), but his popularity among the common people seems to have been extremely widespread (Luke 3:7, Matthew 3:5, Mark 11:32). Indeed, Jesus Himself was able to remind them, "Ye were willing for a season to rejoice in his light" (John 5:35).

---

[1] Sir John Seeley, *Ecce Homo,* Chapter 1.

The angel promised, "He shall be great in the sight of the Lord" (Luke 1:15). Jesus confirmed Gabriel's prediction, "Among them that are born of women, there hath not risen a greater than John the Baptist" (Matthew 11:11).

The coming into the world of one whom God counts great is always cause for gladness. Greatness in God's estimation belongs to those who are linked with His eternal purposes of redemption.

Zacharias was informed that his child would never drink alcoholic beverages of any kind. John was neither a Nazarite nor a Rechabite. The Nazarite vow was for a limited time only (Numbers 6:1-12). It included a ban on shaving and haircutting. It was for a specific purpose. The Rechabites were forbidden to live in houses. They were not allowed to cultivate the land (Jeremiah 35:6f.). They were obviously a pastoral nomadic tribe. A later Jewish tradition that they intermarried with the Levites and so entered the Temple service may be worthy of consideration.

*   *   *   *   *

From the words of Malachi (3:1, 4:4ff.), the Jews believed that Elijah would return as the herald of the Messiah. It required the explanation of Jesus to open the eyes of His followers on this subject. "This is Elijah which was to come" (Matthew 11:14); "Elijah truly shall come first and restore all things. . . . Then the disciples understood that he spake unto them of John the Baptist" (Matthew 17:10ff.).

John's resemblance to Elijah was twofold. They looked alike because they wore the same kind of rough cloth woven from the harsh hair of the camel (2 Kings 1:8, Matthew 3:4). They had the same message of stern rebuke and invitation to repentance (1 Kings 18:21, 21:20, Luke 3:7f.).

It was God who visited His people when Jesus came. John was to "go before him" (Luke 1:17), to prepare "the way of the Lord" (Luke 3:4).

John was born six months before Jesus (Luke 1:26, 56). His descent was priestly on both sides. His parents were among those who took to heart the words of the Law, "These words, which I command thee this day, shall be upon thine heart: and thou shalt teach them diligently unto thy children, and shalt talk of them when thou sittest in thine house, and when thou walkest by the way, and when thou liest down, and when thou risest up" (Deuteronomy 6:6f.).

Chapter Ten

BETHLEHEM

"Let us now go even unto Bethlehem" (Luke 2:15) is the song of Christmas. Bethlehem is the best loved spot in all the world. There is a holy moment every year when the unity of the Church is revealed, in Bethlehem.

If earth and heaven can combine, if angels and men can agree, it surely ought not to be surprising that men can get together for one brief hour. Theologians and ecclesiastics forget their differences. Orthodox, Reformed, Episcopalian and Free surmount the barriers which separate them in worship. "All who profess and call themselves Christians," if they will lay aside every weight, and come as *pilgrims* to Bethlehem, will find there common ground, common cause, common faith, and common hope.

The word "Bethlehem" means "House of Bread." It is not irrelevant that the birth of Jesus was associated with such a name. He fed the multitudes (Matthew 14:13ff., Mark 6:32ff., Luke 9:10 ff., John 6:1ff. This is the only miracle recorded by all four Evangelists.). He taught His followers to pray, "Give us this day our daily bread" (Matthew 6:11, Luke 11:3). One of His great claims was, "I am the bread of life" (John 6:35).

The *Bread of Life* has been disseminated from Bethlehem to all parts of the world. It is the only Bread which satisfies the hunger of the soul (John 6:35). Because all need it, it is the Bread which may be bought "without money and without price" (Isaiah 55:1).

When the Emperor Hadrian crushed the Jewish revolt in A.D. 132, he singled out the centers of Christian and Jewish devotion for complete destruction. Among them were the sites of the Crucifixion and the Resurrection, and the town of Bethlehem. He applied a scorched-earth policy to David's town. His soldiers ploughed the ruins into the soil, and planted a grove to Adonis. This shows that even before A.D. 132 Bethlehem was famous as a place of Christian pilgrimage. The Fourth Evangelist takes it for granted that his readers know the story of the birth of Jesus in Bethlehem (John 7:41f.).

*   *   *   *   *

In the Old Testament, Bethlehem is called "Ephrath" (Genesis 48:7), or "Ephratah" (Micah 5:2), an epithet given it because of its fruitfulness. It was formerly a stronghold of the Jebusites (2 Samuel 5:7, 9, 1 Chronicles 11:5, 7).

Bethlehem appears in the Old Testament chiefly, but not exclusively, in connection with the house of David. It was probably never of very great importance, although it is suggested that at one time the Tabernacle rested in its fields (Psalm 132:6f.). It is remarkable that David did nothing for Bethlehem because he retained affection for it (2 Samuel 23:15).

Rachel, Jacob's dearly beloved wife, died in childbirth near Bethlehem. Jacob mourned for her and erected a pillar over her grave (Genesis 35:16ff.). Rachel's Tomb is still shown today, a little outside the city where the road to Bethlehem turns off from the main thoroughfare. The Crusaders of the twelfth century built a domed structure over the "Twelve Stones" put there by Jacob to represent the Twelve Tribes of Israel.

The love idyll of Ruth, the most exquisite story in the Old Testament, found its consummation in Bethlehem. When Naomi persuaded Orpah to return to her own land, Moab, Ruth uttered the most beautiful confession of love in all literature, "Intreat me not to leave thee, or to return from following after thee: for whither thou goest, I will go; and whither thou lodgest, I will lodge: thy people shall be my people, and thy God my God: Where thou diest, will I die, and there will I be buried: the Lord do so to me, and more also, if aught but death part thee and me" (Ruth 1:16f.).

Ruth could not foresee that she would find acceptance in Bethlehem. She could not foresee that she would marry the good man Boaz. She could not foresee that she would hold in her arms a son who was to be the father of Jesse and the grandfather of David. Far less could she foresee the Child that was to be born in Bethlehem of Judea in the days of Herod the king, with some of her blood in His veins and some of her qualities in His heart. She knew none of these things. She struggled on to Bethlehem motivated only by love.

Samuel journeyed to Bethlehem to anoint the youthful David

to be the successor of King Saul (1 Samuel 16:1ff.). David was the youngest son of Jesse, and the grandson of Obed who was the son of Ruth and Boaz. David was a shepherd in the fields of Bethlehem, where he killed a lion and a bear (1 Samuel 13:34).

The Philistine marauders captured Bethlehem during the turbulent days of the early kingdom, and David was hard pressed by them. While hiding in a nearby cave, he expressed a desire for a drink of water from the well near the city gates of Bethlehem. "Three mighty men brake through the host of the Philistines, and drew water out of the well of Bethlehem" for thé king. When he realized they had risked their lives in this way, he felt the water was too precious to drink, and he poured it out as an offering to God (2 Samuel 23:14ff.).

The Old Testament expressly states that Bethlehem is to be the birthplace of the Messiah (Micah 5:2). The Jews never questioned this. They never doubted the literal fulfillment of this prophecy (Matthew 2:6, John 7:42).

❋   ❋   ❋   ❋   ❋

Bethlehem is situated on the eastern brow of a ridge that runs from east to west, overlooking the great highway from Jerusalem to Hebron and Egypt. It is about five miles south of the capital. From the highest point — 2,537 feet — there is an extensive view towards Jericho. The Dead Sea is in plain sight, shimmering at the foot of the long blue wall of the mountains of Moab beyond.

Around Bethlehem there are great barren regions. Below it is the long grim wilderness of Sinai. Beyond the harsh ramparts of Moab, the formidable desert stretches away to the deep heart of Asia. To the west of the Jordan Valley, there is the gaunt and lonely expanse from which the mighty prophet Amos emerged. A stone donkey-path descends from the edge of Bethlehem to the wild country of Tekoa, which was his home (Amos 1:1).

Closer to Bethlehem, there was a kindlier terrain. Wheat and barley ripened in the fields (Ruth 1:22, 2:23). Figs, almonds, olives, pomegranates, and grapes grew in profusion on the extensive terraces. The wine of Bethlehem was among the best in Palestine.

When Jesus was born, Bethlehem was a sleepy market town. The bustle and confusion of the enrollment soon passed, and it returned to its normal quiet existence.

It is a singular instance of the irony of history that when Rome was sacked by Alaric and his Visigoth hordes on August 24, A.D. 410, some of its noblest patrician families fled to Bethlehem, where they found refuge. In the holy town where her imperial pride had given the Lord of Glory a manager for a cradle, a remnant of her people found shelter in the day of her calamity.

Bethlehem today is a neglected Jordan village. It is forgotten —except at Christmas. It has a population of about ten thousand. It is still a quiet market town for those who don't want the bother of traveling the short distance to Jerusalem. The houses which have been built within the last two hundred years are no different from those which were there when Jesus came. The streets are still too narrow for vehicular traffic.

Working with mother-of-pearl was introduced as a cottage industry in the sixteenth century. Because of the sentimental attachment, there is a constant demand for religious articles such as prayer books, crosses, and the like which have been decorated in Bethlehem.

Chapter Eleven

THE STABLE

There fared a mother driven forth
Out of an inn to roam;
In the place where she was homeless
All men are at home.
The crazy stable close at hand,
With shaking timber and shifting sand,
Grew a stronger thing to abide and stand
Than the square stones of Rome.
— G. K. Chesterton

A British soldier who had fought under the Duke of Wellington in his campaigns against Napoleon lived to be a very old man. Toward the end of his life, he was taken to see Lady Butler's famous painting, "The Square at Quatre Bras," which was one of the battles in which he had seen action.

As he looked at the picture, with its serried ranks of red coated soldiers, he slowly shook his head. Then he said, "It didn't look like that to us. You see, the lady who painted that picture was looking at us from the outside. All we could see were the faces of the Frenchmen coming at us. No sir! It didn't look like that to us."

If we make the pilgrimage to the birthplace of Jesus, we shall find it a place of disillusionment. We have looked at it for too long "from the outside."

We have been grossly misled and misinformed by sentimental and spurious "Nativity Scenes." The Great Masters, and their unknown counterparts who design Christmas cards, have all been guilty of looking "from the outside."

Many of us imagine that when Jesus was born, conditions were almost idyllic. Perhaps this impression is due in part to the pastoral emphasis. To a larger degree, however, it is due to our failure to read the New Testament intelligently.

Politically, Palestine was seething with unrest. Economically, the great masses of the poor were getting poorer and the few rich were getting richer. Socially, there was a great chasm between the highly educated Scribes, Pharisees, Sadducees, and Herodians on the one hand, and "the people of the land," as they contemptuously called them, on the other. The only thing which united the Jews was their common hatred of Rome.[1] At this particular time, their grumbling was against the "decree of Caesar Augustus that all the world should be enrolled" (Luke 2:1).

In obedience to the mandate of Caesar, Mary and Joseph went south. But Caesar was simply the executor of a Higher Will, the Will that moves silently but surely back of all thrones and principalities and powers.

They came to Bethlehem. It was a one-horse town. Its solitary street was cobbled with round black stones. They were hard on the feet. They harbored refuse. They caused many a stranger to stumble with a stubbed toe.

❖   ❖   ❖   ❖   ❖

Inns, or *khans*, were usually quite crude affairs. They consisted of a series of thatched rooms built around a central courtyard. Often they were no more than covered porches. The travelers brought their own food for man and beast. They brought the pot in which to cook it on an open fire in the yard. They brought their bedding, and often their firewood. They looked to the innkeeper for water and shelter.

The lone inn of Bethlehem was a shabby sort of place. It blended with its surroundings. Both had seen better days. The inn was extremely old. It may have been the one built by Chimham, who was one of David's favorites (2 Samuel 19:37ff.). If so, Jeremiah tells us it was the place where the murderers of Gedaliah rested on their flight into Egypt (Jeremiah 41:17).

For many centuries there was an inn built on land which belonged to the family of David. It was widely known as "The Inn of Chimham." Legend said it occupied the exact site of the house where David was born. If that old story is true, it throws new light on the events we are considering, and gives added significance to some of them.

When Mary and Joseph reached Bethlehem, no one took any

[1] It is by no means certain that the Herodians can be included in this generalization. Many of them were "collaborators."

notice of them. They were lost in a milling crowd of nameless ones. None of them had wanted to come. Some of them decided to make the best of their compulsory vacation. They had not tasted the good rich wine of Bethlehem for a long time and there was plenty on hand. They were too busy with their conviviality to pay any attention to stragglers and strangers.

Like most of the men, Joseph wore crude sandals which were made of castoff rope. They were the badge of the poor. Mary was barefooted. It is usually assumed that she rode on a donkey. There is no evidence for this, but I hope it is correct. While it is true that under normal conditions even a pregnant Eastern woman would have to walk while her lord and master rode, we may be sure that Joseph was anxious to protect "that holy thing" (Luke 1:35) carried by his wife.

The innkeeper took one look at them, and when he said, "No room," he meant it. The poets, as well as the painters, have led us astray here.

> *There was a gentle hostler*
> *(And blessed be his name!)*
> *He opened up the stable*
> *The night Our Lady came.*
> *Our Lady and Saint Joseph,*
> *He gave them food and bed,*
> *And Jesus Christ has given him*
> *A glory round his head.*
>
> —Joyce Kilmer

This is sentimentality of the worst kind. It does not correspond to any of the facts in our possession.

The innkeeper turned them away. Joseph had to lead the weary donkey to a common stable. Those who have seen an Eastern byre, retch at the thought. There was no trace of the sapphire mist, or the scent of sandalwood, of which sentiment is so fond. It was full of insects with shrill voices. The loathsome blueflies gorged themselves on offal. Neither door nor curtain covered the opening of the cave.

The grotto that is now shown as the Lord's birthplace is in the southeast section of the town. The tradition that connects this particular cave with His birth is very ancient. It reaches back at least to the middle of the second century. Justin Martyr (A.D.

150) mentions it, and so does Origen, who lived a hundred years later.

The Scriptures, Josephus, and many authorities speak of the numerous caves which are found throughout Palestine, and of the different uses to which they were put in Bible times.

They were used for dwellings (Genesis 19:30). The Horites were prehistoric cave-dwellers, who lived in Seir (Genesis 14:6, Deuteronomy 2:12, 22, etc.). People in terror fled to hide themselves in caves (Isaiah 2:19, Revelation 2:15). Outlaws made caves their headquarters (1 Samuel 22:1). The persecuted found refuge in them (1 Kings 18:4). Farmers used them for shelter against marauders (Judges 6:2). Caves were commonly used for burial places (Genesis 23:19, John 11:38, 19:41). They were also used as dungeons (Jeremiah 37:16f.). The common phrase, "den of robbers" (Jeremiah 7:11, Matthew 21:13), indicates another use to which ancient caves were put. They were used as pens for dangerous beasts (Daniel 6:7).

There were many very extensive caves in Palestine. One is mentioned which could hold six hundred men (Judges 20:47). The famous Cave of Adullam (1 Samuel 21:1f.) was a series of caverns in which it was possible to get lost.

A new interest in old caves has been created by the discovery of the Dead Sea Scrolls. Near a valley called "Wadi Qumran," at the northwest corner of the Dead Sea, more than ten caves have yielded Hebrew and Aramaic manuscripts of great antiquity. Some of them are portions of the Old Testament, a thousand years older than anything scholars have hitherto known.

❊   ❊   ❊   ❊   ❊

In religion, anything mechanical is false. God did not "wave a wand" and magically provide marvelous lodgings for the needy travelers. He who "measured the waters in the hollow of his hand, and meted out the heavens with a span" (Isaiah 40:12),

> *. . . laid His glory by,*
> *He wrapped Him in our clay;*
> *Unmarked by human eye,*
> *The latent Godhead lay;*
> *Infant of days He here became,*
> *And bore the mild Immanuel's name.*
> —Charles Wesley

O strange indifference!—low and high
Drowsed over common joys and cares:
The earth was still—but knew not why;
The world was listening—unawares;
How calm a moment may precede
One that shall thrill the world for ever !
To that still moment, none would heed,
Man's doom was linked, no more to sever,
In the solemn midnight
Centuries ago.

It is the calm and solemn night!
A thousand bells ring out and throw
Their joyous peals abroad, and smite
The darkness, charm'd and holy now!
The night that erst no name had worn,
To it a happy name is given;
For in that stable lay new-born
The peaceful Prince of Earth and Heaven,
In the solemn midnight
Centuries ago.

—Alfred Domett

He who ended in a cave, the sepulcher of Joseph of Arimathea (Luke 23:50ff.), also began in a cave. Neither was unforeseen. Neither was "an emergency." God is big enough—even for Christmas!

When Mary "brought forth her firstborn son" in all the discomfort and inconvenience of a stable, she "wrapped him in swaddling clothes" (Luke 2:7).

A Jewish baby was often sprinkled with salt at birth, after his initial washing (Ezekiel 16:4). Then the arms were laid at his side, and he was wrapped snugly in bandages. This was supposed to strengthen him. Such were the "swaddling clothes" in which the newborn Jesus was wrapped.

Then Mary laid Him in "a manger." This was a feeding trough used by animals. It was probably a hollowed-out stone. It was heavy enough so that the cattle could not push it around or upset it. To turn the manger into a crib was a simple matter for Mary. Nothing more was needed than a supply of clean hay and, we may suppose, some sort of cloth with which to cover it.

Hay! hay did you say?
Surely it was not hay
On which the Christ-Child lay?
Humble indeed the shed,
Awkward the manger bed,
Was there no linen spread?
Come, was it hay you said?

Yes, it was common hay,
Cut on a summer's day . . .
As the sweet crop they drest—
Dividing good from best—
They knew not some would rest
This world's most holy Guest.
                              —Anonymous

There is a lovely old folk tale which says that on the day when the Lord Jesus was born, there was a little brown creature awake in the hay. He saw the Shepherds come with their simple offerings of bread and milk. He watched the resplendent Wise Men bring their costly gifts. He wanted with all his heart to do something for the newborn Saviour. But what could he do?

At last he thought of something within his power. Clutching hold of a specially fragrant piece of hay, he pushed, carried, and dragged it, with a tremendous struggle, to the manger. There he added it to the hay on which the Baby Jesus lay.

Just as he did so, the Baby smiled, stretched out His hand, and touched him. Immediately the little brown thing began to glow with light. Ever since, the glowworms, whose faraway ancestor wanted so much to serve Jesus, and finally found a way, have shone in the darkness.

The coming of Jesus has made a greater difference to the history of mankind than any other event that has ever happened. Yet when He came, not only was there no one to welcome Him, there were few even to recognize Him.

They had no room for Him,
No handkerchief to fold under His head,
No old coat to throw over His bed.
The candle flickered and grew dim,
Her shadow leapt and dwindled over Him;
And in her shadow's dance

The secret hosts advance.
Angels are there, philosophers and kings,
Herdsmen, artificers of humble things,
Hidden behind His mother, on the floor
Of mud and clay they drop down to adore.
—George Every

❋   ❋   ❋   ❋   ❋

It is interesting that in the New Testament Bethlehem is never mentioned as having been visited by our Lord. It is in no way associated with His ministry. Its sole claim to fame is that it was the place of His birth. Today, no *Jews* live there. It is repugnant to them for the very reason which makes it sacred to Christians. On every hand Bethlehem reveals the touch of Christ.

Cradled in a manger, meanly
Laid the Son of Man His head;
Sleeping His first earthly slumber
Where the oxen had been fed.
—George Stringer Rowe

Were earth a thousand times as fair,
Beset with gold and jewels rare,
She yet were far too poor to be
A narrow cradle, Lord, for Thee.
—Martin Luther

Chapter Twelve

JOSEPH

Joseph was the husband of Mary. It was commonly assumed that he was the father of Jesus (Luke 3:23).

Matthew is careful to state that Joseph belonged to the royal line of David, through Solomon. In the opening verses of his gospel he traces his ancestry back to Abraham. In Joseph's first dream, the angel addressed him as the "son of David" (Matthew 1:20). Luke also classifies him as "of the house of David" (Luke 2:4).

Joseph is not mentioned in Mark's gospel. John introduces him on two occasions only. Each time it is done indirectly. Philip speaks to Nathaniel of "Jesus of Nazareth, the son of Joseph" (John 1:45). When the Jews become infuriated with Jesus for describing Himself as the Bread which came down from heaven, they scoff, "Is not this Jesus, the son of Joseph?" (John 6:42).

Joseph was a carpenter. It was not an honored trade. When His own people were offended in Jesus because they thought He was beginning to "forget his place," they sought to cut Him down to size with the scornful words, "Is not this the carpenter's son?" (Matthew 13:55). They may have had in mind the words of Sirach, "How can he get wisdom that holdeth the plow? . . . so every carpenter and workman that laboreth night and day. . . . they shall not sit high in the congregation. . . . and they shall not be found where parables are spoken" (Ecclesiasticus 38:25-34).

The village carpenter was not a skilled artisan. The fond idea that Joseph was a master craftsman who smoothed and polished exotic woods into beautiful furniture has no basis in fact. All he made for houses were crude doors set in primitive frames, and roof beams so rough he seldom was careful to strip off all the bark.

He fashioned a few simple necessities for the peasant farmer. He made yokes for the ox and the mule. He searched the mountains above the pasture land for straight saplings. He sharpened one end and passed them on to the blacksmith who "shod" them with tips of iron. This transformed them into the most primitive of plows.

The tools of a village carpenter were an adze, which was hammer, chisel and plane in one; a saw; an ax; a bow and drill; and a knife. They indicate the range of his abilities.

* * * * *

Joseph was a poor man. His offering in the Temple shows that. The Law set the Purification Sacrifice as a lamb or a kid (Leviticus 12:6). Those who were unable to meet this requirement brought "a pair of turtledoves, or two young pigeons" (Leviticus 12:8, Luke 2:24).

Joseph lived in the Galilean town of Nazareth. It was situated in a high valley at the southern end of the limestone hills of Lebanon. The magnificent view to the south swept over the historic Plain of Esdraelon as far as the Sea of Galilee. On clear days the sun could be seen shimmering on the waters of the blue Mediterranean in the west. On the northern horizon, old Hermon lifted its hoary head. In the east, the yellow mountains of Gilead rose steeply, providing an awesome backdrop for the green Mount Tabor.

Although it was only a day's journey from Carmel on the coast, or from Capernaum and Tiberias on the Sea of Gennesaret, Nazareth was cut off by the mountains from the rest of the world. It was the abode of genuine hillbillies. They tilled the sparse soil. Their necessities were few. They were out of touch with the political conflicts of Judea. The Romans left them alone so long as they paid their taxes.

Nazareth was so obscure and unimportant, it is not even mentioned in the Old Testament. It was so far off the beaten path, and so unessential to the national life, that it had become a byword throughout Palestine (John 1:46). It was just another outpost, sleeping among the quiet hills.

* * * * *

Joseph was "a just man" (Matthew 1:19). This means several things. It indicates he was a strict observer not only of the Law, but also of the Feasts. He went to Jerusalem every year to celebrate the Passover in the Temple (Luke 2:41). However, when Matthew says he was "a just man," he gives the word a much

wider and nobler significance. He means what we mean today
when we speak warmly of someone as "a *good* man."

The Law gave an engaged man the right to condemn an un-
faithful partner to death by stoning (Deuteronomy 22:23f.). This
ancient code had been softened a little through the years by the
Pharisees. They preferred divorce to death. The Sadducees still
insisted on the letter of the Law. Joseph was evidently as en-
lightened as he was merciful. He decided on the less painful
course of action.

There were two ways of obtaining a divorce. The accused
could be dragged before a "town meeting." There her shame was
broadcast to all. She was publicly accused of infidelity. The details were not spared. The witnesses had a field day. Then the
injured party repudiated her in front of all the gossips and curiosity seekers.

Provision, however, was made for private proceedings. The
man handed the woman a bill of divorcement in the presence of
two witnesses. When Joseph discovered Mary was pregnant, he
chose to do this (Matthew 1:19). He wished to spare her feelings
as much as possible. He was "a good man."

*   *   *   *   *

A carpenter is usually considered to be a sober, matter-of-
fact, down-to-earth person. He is not commonly credited with
special visionary characteristics. Yet in the brief delineation of
Joseph, we are told he had four dreams in which an angel
brought him messages from God.

In the first dream (Matthew 1:20f.), the angel had a fourfold
exhortation. (1) Joseph was to go through with his intention to
marry Mary. (2) She was innocent of any wrongdoing, for she
was with child by the Holy Spirit. (3) Joseph was to name the
Child "Jesus." (4) The purpose of this mystery was to be fulfilled
in the mission and ministry of Jesus, who would "save his people
from their sins." It is hard to believe that Joseph understood all
the implications. Nevertheless, he "was not disobedient to the
heavenly vision."

The second dream occurred after the visit of the Wise Men
(Matthew 2:13). Joseph was instructed to take Jesus and Mary
to Egypt. This was to thwart the evil plans of Herod. They were
to stay in Egypt until the death of the king.

The third dream happened on the death of Herod (Matthew
2:19). The angel appeared to Joseph while the Holy Family was

staying in Egypt. He was informed it was safe to return home. "Home" was apparently Bethlehem. While they were making the journey, they learned that Archelaus was reigning in Judea in the place of his father, Herod. Joseph "was afraid" to return to Judea. He dreaded the new king, whose character was notorious. Archelaus had all the bad qualities of his father, without the redeeming feature of his exalted mental powers. He was utterly unscrupulous. He had no regard for the sanctity of human life. For nine miserable years he misruled the Jews. In A.D. 6 he was deposed by Caesar Augustus and banished to Vienne in Gaul. "Being warned of God in a dream" (Matthew 2:22), Joseph led his family into Galilee. Antipas, a brother of Archelaus, was Tetrarch of Galilee. He could be tyrannical too, but he was more interested in debauchery than murder.

❋   ❋   ❋   ❋   ❋

It was from Nazareth that Joseph and Mary took Jesus to Jerusalem when He was twelve years of age (Luke 2:41ff.). It was to Nazareth that they returned after that exacting visit. They lived in Nazareth, where Jesus "was subject unto them." For all practical purposes, Joseph was the earthly father of Jesus.

We do not know how long this continued. The tradition that Joseph died and Jesus had to support His widowed Mother and her family, is both ancient and widespread. It is supported by the suggestive phrase "Is not this the carpenter?" (Mark 6:3). If Joseph had been alive on that occasion, he would surely have been named with the rest of the family. At the Crucifixion, Jesus charged John to care for His Mother (John 19:6). It would have been an unusual request if Joseph still lived.

The myth that Joseph was a widower with children by a former wife, was invented in the interest of the dogma of Mary's perpetual virginity. It is certainly not supported by such evidence as we have in the New Testament. "Is not this the carpenter's son? is not his mother called Mary? and his brethren James, and Joses, and Simon, and Judas? And his sisters, are they not all with us?" (Matthew 13:55f.). This is a plain, straightforward statement. The attempt to change "brothers" and "sisters" into "stepbrothers" and "stepsisters," or even "cousins," is completely unjustified. No one who is prepared to allow the Greek record *to speak for itself* can entertain such notions. "When history gives us brothers, and Dogma says they must be cousins—in any other case the decision of the historian would be clear, and so it is here."[1]

"And [he] knew her not till she had brought forth her firstborn son" (Matthew 1:25). This verse contains two plain assumptions. First, he *did* "know her" after the birth of Jesus. Otherwise the statement is unnecessary. Indeed, it is meaningless. Secondly, the use of the word "firstborn" implies that afterwards she had other children. Whenever the New Testament refers to the brothers of Jesus, it gives the impression they were younger than He.

We know nothing of the end of Joseph. We are not told when, where, or how he died. He drops out of the picture at an early stage.

He must have been "a good man." True goodness is always unconscious of itself. It reached a rare degree of excellence in him, because Jesus called God "Father," and *His conception of fatherhood was shaped, in part at least, by Joseph.*

---

[1] T. R. Glover, *The Jesus of History*, p. 26.

Chapter Thirteen

THE CHOSEN WOMAN
OF THE CHOSEN RACE

"There is one God, and one mediator between God and men, the man Christ Jesus" (1 Timothy 2:5). We must always remember this. Nothing we say about the Blessed Mother of our Lord must be allowed to detract one iota from the glory and the majesty, the dominion and the power, which are His alone.

It is difficult, if not impossible, for us to form an unbiased estimate of Mary. As Protestants, we are conditioned against her by what we consider to be the excesses of Rome. This does not, however, justify us in going to the other extreme. We cannot lightly dismiss her as "just another woman." She was the Mother of our Lord. Elisabeth was not joking when she said, "Blessed art thou among women" (Luke 1:42). The angel attributed to her even greater honor, "Thou hast found favor with God" (Luke 1:30). If Protestants were representative of Christians in every age, to what extent would the prophecy be fulfilled, "From If we put the prejudices out of our minds, along with what we henceforth all generations shall call me blessed"? (Luke 1:48). consider to be the extravagances of others, it may be that we shall come to regard her as the most beautiful character in the Bible.

Unfortunately, the gospels are extremely reticent about Mary. She is obscured from us by a veil of hymns and prayers, visions and visitations. We catch but a fleeting glimpse here and there. No doubt this is why some have exalted her above measure, and others have neglected her without reason.

The silence of the gospels is more than adequately compensated by the fullness of tradition. The apocryphal gospels inform us that she was the daughter of Joachim and Anna. Her father is described as a Galilean who lived in Nazareth. It is said that her mother was a Judean, hailing from Bethlehem. We are further told that at the time she was engaged to Joseph, she was between twelve and fourteen years of age.

Only one other member of her immediate family is mentioned in the pages of the New Testament. That is her sister (John 19:25). She was probably Salome, the wife of Zebedee, the mother of James and John. This would account for Salome's continued interest in the welfare of Jesus and His disciples (Mark 15:40f., 16:1). It would also help to explain her brashness in asking Jesus to make James and John the chief officials in His Kingdom (Matthew 20:20ff.). She wanted to keep as much in the family as she could!

Papias, who was a disciple of John, states that Mary had two sisters, Mary the wife of Cleopas, and Mary the wife of Zebedee. Three sisters with identical names is a little too much.

Nowhere in Scripture are we explicitly told that Mary belonged to the royal household. Yet everywhere the New Testament insists that Jesus was "the son of David." It is not interested in any legal definition, such as might be possible through adoption by Joseph.

On the Day of Pentecost, Peter declared that in Jesus God fulfilled the oath which He sware to David, "that of the fruit of his loins according to the flesh he would raise up Christ to sit on his throne" (Acts 2:30). When this statement is placed alongside the original promise, "I will set up thy seed after thee which shall proceed out of thy bowels" (2 Samuel 7:12), it points to Jesus as the lineal descendant of David.

The words of Paul readily bear the same interpretation. "Of this man's seed hath God according to his promise raised unto Israel a Saviour, Jesus" (Acts 13:23), "which was made of the seed of David according to the flesh" (Romans 1:3). "Remember that Jesus Christ of the seed of David was raised from the dead" (2 Timothy 2:8).

The author of the Epistle to the Hebrews asserts, "For it is evident that our Lord sprang out of Judah" (Hebrews 7:14). The Bible closes with the proclamation, "I Jesus have sent mine angel to testify unto you these things in the churches. I am the root and offspring of David" (Revelation 22:16).

The words of the angel to Mary, "the Lord shall give unto him the throne of his father David" (Luke 1:32), indicate that, *as her Son*, He was "the son of David." It was therefore the general belief of the New Testament Church that Mary belonged to the royal line.

The family of the Virgin was connected in some way with that of Elisabeth, the mother of John the Baptist (Luke 1:36). The exact relationship cannot be determined. The translation "cousin" is a mistake. The Revised Version of 1881 corrected this error. It was wisely followed by Dr. Moffatt, the Revised Standard Version, and the New English Bible, all of which give "kinswoman."

Elisabeth was descended from a long line of priests (Luke 1:5). If Mary enjoyed the same ancestry, the regal and the priestly strains met in her. At any rate, she possessed the dignity of the one and the sanctity of the other.

      ❋   ❋   ❋   ❋   ❋

Mary is introduced as a maiden of Nazareth in Galilee (Luke 1:26f.). Her family must have been a humble one to arrange a marriage for her with a carpenter. There were no unions in those days. A carpenter's lot was a hard one.

The artists' conceptions of her clothed in gorgeous raiment are far from the truth. She dressed in coarse, unbleached linen, with a dark-blue headband about her brow, after the manner of Galilean peasants.

She was "a virgin espoused to a man whose name was Joseph" (Luke 1:27). At betrothal, an engagement ring was given to the prospective bride. This is an extremely ancient custom. It probably dates back to Egypt before the days of Moses. At a time when literacy was rare, a party to an agreement "sealed" the contract with his stamp. It was then an unbreakable pact. From the time of the formal betrothal, which was made in the presence of witnesses, the bride wore the bridegroom's ring. It was his "sign," his "seal."

This ancient ritual is known as *subarrhation*. It was a notable occasion. When an engagement had been made in this manner, it could be terminated only by divorce. An espoused woman was regarded as already married. If her fiancé died during their engagement, she was considered to be a widow.

It was while Mary was engaged to Joseph (Luke 1:27) that the angel Gabriel appeared to her in Nazareth (Luke 1:26ff.). He told her God wanted her to be the Mother of the Messiah.

Apart from the gracious manner in which she received this wonderful news, the mere fact that it came to *her* illuminates her character for us. God does not choose His agents at random. We must believe that Mary was, of all women, the best suited for this sublime task. *She was the Chosen Woman of the Chosen*

Race. Hers was the one heart in all the world to whose love, authority and strength God was willing to entrust His only begotten Son.

Mary did not ask the angel for proof as Zacharias did (Luke 1:18). The simple question, "How shall this be, seeing I know not a man?" (Luke 1:34) is the spontaneous reaction of a Virgin conscious of her own purity. It is drawn from her by the strange declaration that she is to bear a son before her marriage is consummated.

Nevertheless, a sign is given. The fact that Elisabeth is to have a child in her old age shows that "with God nothing shall be impossible" (Luke 1:36).

The angel makes her a promise, "He shall be great, and shall be called the Son of the Most High: and the Lord God shall give unto him the throne of his father David: and he shall reign over the house of Jacob for ever; and of his kingdom there shall be no end" (Luke 1:32f.). In these momentous words her coming Son is identified as the Messiah, the "Hope of Israel," in whom all the prophecies shall be fulfilled.

The modest statement with which Mary accepts the role assigned to her, "Behold, the handmaid of the Lord; be it unto me according to thy word" (Luke 1:38) is of deep spiritual significance to every believer.

Mary would never have heard the Divine messenger if she had not longed to do the Divine Will. By her full and eager co-operation with the eternal purpose of God, she entered into "the joy of the Lord" more completely than any other member of the human family.

Yet it was not an unmixed joy. When the infant Jesus was brought into the Temple (Luke 2:22), Simeon recognized Him as the Lord's Anointed. In his exultation, he blessed God and he blessed them. Then he turned to Mary, and addressed her in words which are as solemn as any in the New Testament, "Behold, this child is set for the fall and rising again of many in Israel; and for a sign which shall be spoken against; (yea, a sword shall pierce through thine own soul also,) that the thoughts of many hearts may be revealed" (Luke 2:34f.).

The somber words of the seer did not indicate something from which Mary had been delicately sheltered. After the angel had made the Annunciation to her, Mary had journeyed to an unspecified town in Judea, to visit her kinswoman Elisabeth (Luke 1:39). She stayed there for three months, probably until

John the Baptist was born. She then returned to Nazareth (Luke 1:56).

Her condition could no longer be hid. The integrity of this peerless maiden was put to a severe test. The town gossips hurled their venomed shafts from every side. You can hear them, can't you? "There was something not quite *kosher* about that trip she claimed to have made to Elisabeth—by herself! a likely tale!" "How fast and loose she played with that poor man Joseph!" "And now the jackass is even talking about marrying her!" And so they went on.

In their myopic eyes she was the bearer of sin and shame. But to the eyes of innocence and faith, she bore Him who came to bear away man's sin and shame.

And so she magnified the Lord as He grew big within her, and prepared to deliver to the sneering world its hallowed Deliverer.

*   *   *   *   *

When Jesus was twelve years old, the sword of which Simeon had spoken pricked her. It did not pierce her soul, but it reminded her of the good man's words.

Jesus stayed behind in the Temple when Mary and Joseph began their return journey to Nazareth. It was almost in panic that they hastily retraced their steps looking for Him. After searching frantically for three days, they eventually found Him. In exasperation Mary inquired, "Son, why hast thou dealt thus with us?" His answer was dramatically brief and pointed, "Wist ye not that I must be about my Father's business?" "They understood not the saying which he spake unto them" (Luke 2:46ff.). How could they? For twelve years they had known Him as an obedient Boy, not noticeably different from the rest of the lads.

This is the beginning of the real tragedy of Mary's life. But just as His childhood allayed the fears aroused by Simeon, so the dread of losing Him was eased by the silent years which followed. "He went down with them, and came to Nazareth, and was subject unto them: but his mother kept all these sayings in her heart" (Luke 2:51).

Eighteen years later (Luke 3:23), Jesus left home for good. He was apparently moved by the preaching of John the Baptist. The path He took was not the one His mother expected Him to take. More plainly than ever, she was outside His life.

This was brought home to her in an unmistakable manner when Jesus performed His first miracle at Cana of Galilee (John

2:1ff.). She asked Him to help because they had run out of wine. Whatever her motive, Jesus had to remind her that He was no longer under her jurisdiction. "Woman, what have I to do with thee?" (John 2:4). She had to slip back into the shadows with the servants.

Not long afterward, His unusual behavior caused His friends to worry about His mental condition (Mark 3:21). They communicated their fears to His family. Mary hurried to Capernaum with her other sons, probably with the idea of taking Him home with them for His own good. As He was teaching in a certain house, He was told that His Mother and His brothers were outside. To make plain the nature of His mission once for all, He replied, "Who is my mother, and who are my brethren?" Then, renouncing natural ties, He pointed to His disciples and said, "Behold, my mother and my brethren" (Mark 3:34).

We read those remarkable sentences carelessly. We hug ourselves and think how wonderful it is we have a part in His family. But how did His words sound to His Mother? Was not her own Son piercing her with a sword? Not even the Mother of Jesus could count her motherhood for anything from this time forth. Strangers were closer to Him than she was. Were not Simeon's words justified? Yet painful as this was for Mary, it was doubly painful for Jesus.

All the gospel writers tell us there were women at the Crucifixion (Matthew 27:55f., Mark 15:40f., Luke 23:49). Only the Fourth Evangelist includes the Virgin Mary with the others: "There stood by the cross of Jesus his mother" (John 19:25). He can say no more than that. It is a scene for the painter rather than the preacher.

In His last moments, in extreme agony, Jesus knit again the bond of natural affection which, at times (but see Mark 7:10ff.) had appeared to be of no account in His eyes. In the Beloved Disciple, He gave to His Mother a son to take the place of Him she was losing. He gave to John what was dearest to Him on earth. "Woman, behold thy son. Behold thy mother" (John 19:26f.).

The final New Testament reference to Mary occurs after the Resurrection and Ascension of Jesus. She was in the Upper Room with the disciples and the brothers of Jesus, waiting for the Day of Pentecost (Acts 1:14).

Earlier we are told, "Neither did his brethren believe in him" (John 7:5). It is usually assumed that the Resurrection changed their minds. It is likely their Mother had something to do with it. At any rate, our last glimpse of the Holy Family finds them united—in Him.

❖   ❖   ❖   ❖   ❖

We do not know what happened to Mary after that. There are two traditions. At least one of them must be wrong. It may well be that both are.

The older story says Mary continued to live in Jerusalem with the Apostle John and that she died there in her fifty-ninth year.

A later tradition, which originated in Ephesus in the fifth century, says she accompanied the Beloved Disciple to that city, where she eventually died and was buried. The difficulties and problems associated with John's residence in that city can be overcome only if we allow that he visited Ephesus in his extreme old age, and did not stay there very long. This makes it unlikely that Mary was still alive, or, if she were alive, would be in any condition to undertake such a journey. The fact that the legend cannot be traced further back than the fifth century weakens it considerably.

The Early Church had a special Feast honoring "The Mother of God." It was celebrated on August 15. It commemorated her death. In its origin, it was nothing more than a "Memorial Service."

In the seventh century, this ritual made its way to Rome. There it was observed under the title "The Falling-Asleep of the Mother of God." Before long, the name was changed to "The Assumption." It took considerably longer to change the content of the ritual from that of a Memorial Service to that of a resurrection. It was not until the Middle Ages that the doctrine was widely accepted in the Latin Church. It was not until A.D. 1950 that Pope Pius XII declared that it was "revealed" and, therefore, an essential part of Roman theology.

There are many different versions of the Assumption legend. The Egyptian story says the event took place 206 days after her death. Most of the other accounts speak of a much shorter period. John of Damascus said Mary's body lay three days in the grave before it was taken up into heaven. Other sources give forty days after her death; others say fifteen days. According to one story, all the Apostles were present at Mary's death except Thomas, who had been summoned from India but was late in arriving. At his request the tomb was opened so that he might pay his last respects to the corpse. The tomb was empty. The Apostles therefore concluded that the body had been taken up to heaven. There are other versions which are pale copies of the story of the Ascension of Jesus. They say the Apostles were actual witnesses of her bodily ascension.

The legend is to be opposed because it is entirely without scriptural or historical evidence. The Festival of the Assumption was unknown in the earliest centuries. It was rejected at the Reformation as being neither primitive nor founded upon any "certain warrant of Holy Scripture."

There are many things we do not know about Mary. But we know some things, perhaps intuitively. She was serenely lovely when she bent over the cradle. She needed no halo, for the light of God was in her soul. She was utterly pathetic when she stood by the Cross. She needed the strong arm of John, for Simeon's prophecy was fulfilled. She was divinely triumphant when she tarried with the disciples, for at last she knew the meaning of His peace.

Mary earned for herself a place in the historic creeds and hymns of the Holy, Catholic and Apostolic Church. When men and women of "all kindreds, and tongues, and people, and nations" confess their faith in the glorious affirmation,

> I believe . . . in Jesus Christ, His only Son, our Lord; Who was conceived by the Holy Ghost, born of the Virgin Mary;

and when they praise God in the sonorous words of the majestic *Te Deum,*

> *When Thou tookest upon Thee to deliver man,*
> *Thou didst not abhor the Virgin's womb,*

Mary is indeed remembered as "blessed among women."

> *Blest in thy lowly heart to store*
> *The homage paid in Bethlehem;*
> *But far more blessed evermore*
> *Thus to have shared the taunts and shame,—*
> *Thus with thy pierc'd heart to have stood*
> *'Mid mocking crowds, and owned Him thine,*
> *True through a world's ingratitude,*
> *And owned in death by lips Divine.*
>
> —Anonymous

Chapter Fourteen

THE VIRGIN BIRTH

It is sometimes argued that because Paul did not formally teach the doctrine of the Virgin Birth, he did not believe it. This, however, is very dangerous logic. If it were applied everywhere, there is hardly a significant Christian dogma it would not affect.

The argument from silence is always precarious. No single New Testament writer mentions every aspect of the Faith. Is it then fair to deduce that those which were not suited to the particular emphasis they sought to make were not believed by them?

Paul's references to the birth of Jesus are to be found in Galatians 4:4, Romans 1:3f., 8:3, and Philippians 2:5ff. An examination of these passages reveals some highly significant information.

In these, and other places, the Apostle to the Gentiles teaches the *pre-existence of Christ*. He magnifies the eternal nature of the eternal Son who was always "in the form of God" (Philippians 2:6), and by whom "all things were created" (Colossians 1:16).

This pre-existent Son was "sent" (Romans 8:3, Galatians 4:4) by the Father. Paul's repeated thesis is that the life of Jesus differs in one respect from every other which has ever been lived on earth. *It did not begin when He was born.* So how could he think of the birth of Jesus in the same way he thought of other births? When he refers specifically to that event, he is careful to state that He was "made of a woman" (Galatians 4:4). He was "made of the seed of David according to the flesh" (Romans 1:3). The context demands that this was the work of God, not of man.

When Paul refers to the nature of Jesus, he deliberately says He is "the Son of God" (2 Corinthians 1:19, Galatians 2:20, Ephesians 4:13, etc.), "his Son" (Romans 1:3, 9; 5:10; 8:3, 32;

etc.), in whom we see "the light of the knowledge of the glory of God" (2 Corinthians 4:6).

On the basis of his remarkable insight into the pre-existent glory and the divine nature of Jesus, we have less cause for rejecting the doctrine of the Virgin Birth than for accepting it.

It is also said that John is silent on this subject, and so does not believe it.

Whether he is "silent on this subject" is open to question. In the usually accepted manuscripts of the Fourth Gospel there is, admittedly, no reference to the Virgin Birth of Jesus. But the manuscripts which we have are late. Several of the church fathers, who wrote earlier than the date of any manuscripts of John which we possess today, seem to have used an older text in which John 1:13 was not plural, as we know it, but singular, so that the passage read, "As many as received him, to them gave he power to become sons of God, even to them that believe in the name of him who was born not of blood, nor of the will of the flesh, nor of the will of man, but of God" (John 1:12f.). If this were the original text, it would certainly invalidate the argument from John's silence.

There are, of course, other considerations. The Fourth Gospel was written with the other three in mind. You cannot understand it unless you remember this. *John presupposes the Synoptics*. It is intelligible on no other terms. Was there, then, any need for him to elaborate on the subject of the Virgin Birth, when he assumed his readers were familiar with the writings of Matthew, Mark and Luke?

It should also be borne in mind that the majestic Prologue to the Fourth Gospel deals with principles. It is not concerned with mechanics. It makes profound statements. It offers no explanations. "In the beginning was the Word. . . . All things were made by him, and without him was not anything made that was made" (John 1:1, 3). How? By what means did He make everything? We are not told. It is outside the writer's scope and purpose. Similarly, when he asserts, "The Word became flesh" (John 1:14), that is all he has to say. He makes a simple statement of fact. He does not try to explain it.

*   *   *   *   *

At the Reformation, many beliefs of the Dark Ages were scrapped. The Reformers did not decide to jettison doctrines according to their personal preferences. The fact that they disliked certain dogmas was not considered sufficient reason for abandoning them.

One group of Reformers took what we might call the negative approach. They said, "We will retain everything not expressly denied by Scripture." The rest of the Reformers took a more positive attitude. They said, "We will retain only what is clearly taught by Scripture." There is a considerable difference.

The doctrine of the Virgin Birth stands up to both these tests. It is not "expressly denied by Scripture." It is "clearly taught by Scripture." It was, therefore, retained by *all* the Reformers as sound Christian doctrine. They never viewed it as one of those tenets which needed "reforming"!

Of course, the dogma of the Virgin Birth is beset with difficulties. But why should this cause *us* trouble? It always has been.

There were tremendous difficulties for Joseph. Yet they were minor compared with the difficulties of Mary. Matthew (1:18ff.) deals with Joseph's dilemma. Luke (1:26ff.) deals with Mary's. Each does so with becoming tact and delicacy. This is appreciated when we compare their accounts with the lurid stories in the Apocryphal Gospels.

The Jews knew of many births which took place only through Divine intervention, such as the birth of Isaac (Genesis 18:11ff.), of Esau and Jacob (Genesis 25:21), and of Samuel (1 Samuel 1:4ff.). There is also the New Testament parallel to these Old Testament incidents, the birth of John the Baptist (Luke 1:13ff.).

The Virgin Birth differs from all these. It is distinct from all other births. It is unique. Jesus had no human father. He was "conceived by the Holy Ghost, born of the Virgin Mary." The birth, but not the parentage, is human. While born of Mary, He is the Son of God.

All four Evangelists testify that Jesus is "the Son of God" (Matthew 8:29, 14:33, 27:54, etc., Mark 1:1, 3:11, etc., Luke 1:35, 4:41, etc., John 1:34, 3:18, 20:31, etc.). John tells us plainly the reason he wrote his gospel was "that ye might believe that Jesus is the Christ, the Son of God" (John 20:31).

      ❋   ❋   ❋   ❋   ❋

If the Virgin Birth were to take place, God in His mercy would not leave Mary in ignorance of the mysterious manner in which He was about to deal with her. The Annunciation to Mary was essential in order to save her from dreadful perplexity and suffering. It was also necessary to secure her co-operation. This was forthcoming in the gentle, unassuming, yet wonderful words, "Behold, the handmaid of the Lord; be it unto me according to thy word" (Luke 1:38).

Mary then visited her kinswoman Elisabeth (Luke 1:39f.). She stayed with her in Judea about three months. When she returned to Nazareth, her condition was obvious to everyone, including Joseph. This was probably the occasion when she informed him of the visit of the angel and of the Divine promise.

Joseph was placed in a very difficult position. He was "a just man." He hesitated to believe her unsupported word. He was equally afraid of condemning her if there was a possibility she was innocent. He therefore decided to "put her away privily" (Matthew 1:19).

It was a great grief to him. No doubt he was more concerned about Mary's future than his own. He was under great pressure from his family, his friends, and the village elders who held him in high esteem. The statement "she was found with child" (Matthew 1:18) suggests a scandal which was not kept discreetly within the family.

It was while Joseph was in this state of mental and emotional confusion that the angel of the Lord appeared to him in a dream (Matthew 1:20). The heavenly messenger confirmed the statement of Mary.

The fact that, in spite of his natural suspicions and the advice of everyone whose opinion he respected, he took her in marriage and solemnly presented her firstborn to God (Luke 2:22ff.), in spite of the clear prohibition of the law regarding illegitimate children (Deuteronomy 23:2), requires us to believe that to Joseph also God had made known His purposes. There is no other rational explanation of Joseph's behavior.

❊　　　❊　　　❊　　　❊　　　❊

The doctrine of the Virgin Birth was part of the Faith of the Early Church. It was accepted by all the recognized authorities of the Patristic era. It was unquestioned by the Reformers. Indeed, it is safe to assert that until the rise of nineteenth-century pseudo-scientific Protestant Liberalism, it was the universal belief of Christendom. The grounds for denying it are purely subjective. On such grounds we can deny anything.

This dogma was given a prominent and permanent place in

the historic creeds of the Church because it embodies two cardinal tenets of the Christian religion.

First, it declares *the one essential belief,* on which every other "Christian" doctrine is based, *that in Jesus Christ God entered human life* "for us men and our salvation." If you deny that, then whatever you may have left, you have destroyed Christianity. Without this belief, the New Testament would never have been written. The supreme evidence for the Virgin Birth is Jesus Himself. He was a fresh start. The first Adam came into the world by the creative act of God. So did the Second Adam. This was God acting for man. It was not man acting for God. This was God taking the initiative. This was God stooping down to man. It was not man reaching up to God. In Jesus Christ, *God* entered human life.

The second fundamental fact emphasized by the doctrine of the Virgin Birth is *the real humanity of Jesus.* The heresies of recent years have attacked the *Divinity* of Jesus. This caused no problem to the first Christians. One of the earliest heresies was a denial of our Lord's *humanity.* Some people called "Docetists" held that Jesus was a Divine being who only *seemed*[1] to be human. The Gnostics developed this idea. They taught that Jesus, during His life on earth, did not have a natural human body, but only an apparent, or phantom, body. All the acts and sufferings of His earthly life, including His Death and Resurrection, were only *apparent.* The Epistles of John were written to combat this heresy (cf. 1 John 2:22, 4:2, 5:6, 20; 2 John 7, etc.).

From the earliest times, the doctrine of the Virgin Birth asserted that Jesus was truly Man as well as truly God.

The Son of God had been conceived by a human Mother who, as the primitive Church read the prophecy of Isaiah 7:14, was a Virgin. It is sometimes argued today that Isaiah's Hebrew word for Virgin, *'almah,* is not the technical one, and may, with equal accuracy, be translated "a young woman of marriageable age." Even if this were correct linguistically, in this case it would be irrelevant. Isaiah does not say, "Behold, *a* virgin shall conceive." He uses the definite article. He says, "Behold, *the* virgin shall conceive." It applies to one person specifically. Further, whatever we think of this verse, we must recognize the meaning it had for the writers of the Nativity Story. From the evidence of their interpretation, we can assume that such was the widespread

---

[1] δοκεῖν, to appear.

belief of their day. Finally, when they translated '*almah* into Greek, they used the word παρθένος—as the translators of the Septuagint did—and it means *virgin* (cf. Matthew 25:1, 7, 11, Acts 21:9, 1 Corinthians 7:25, 28, 34, as well as Luke 1:27).

The Son of God was "conceived by the Holy Ghost" when "the power of the Most High" overshadowed her (Luke 1:35). This is the testimony of Luke the Physician, who had the wisdom to add, "With God nothing shall be impossible" (Luke 1:37). It is a most important addition. It is the basis of everything we believe about miracles in general and the Virgin Birth in particular.

In affirming the miracle of the Virgin Birth, we do not wish to imply that something happened which in any way violated the Divine order of the universe. On the contrary, we insist that it was in perfect harmony with all the other works of God. If God's Will is the ultimate Source of all things, nothing can be "contrary to nature" which happens by that Will. Everything is natural, not to us, but to God. "With God nothing shall be impossible."

While we maintain that the Virgin Birth is not "contrary to nature," we readily admit that it transcends our knowledge of nature. When we remember how limited our knowledge of nature is, this concession is not very difficult to make!

The Evangelists wisely did not vex themselves with metaphysical or scientific questions as to *how* the Virgin Birth was possible, or *how* it actually took place. They were concerned not with its *manner*, but with its *motive,* and this they could understand. They wholeheartedly accepted Paul's great dictum,

"When the fulness of the time was come, God sent forth his Son, made of a woman, made under the law, to redeem them that were under the law, that we might receive the adoption of sons" (Galatians 4:4).

Part Three

Chapter Fifteen

THE SONG OF ELISABETH
Luke 1:42-45

Elisabeth, the wife of Zacharias the godly priest, was just as righteous, devout and dedicated as her husband. He performed the offices of the Temple in good conscience. She pleased Him who "dwelleth not in temples made with hands" (Acts 7:48; cf. 1 Kings 8:27, 2 Chronicles 2:6, 6:18), by living "blameless" before Him at home.

When she discovered she was to have a child in her old age, she "hid herself five months" (Luke 1:24). If she had gone into seclusion for the *last* five months, we might think she was merely following a pattern which was widespread until quite recent times. But Elisabeth remained at home for the *first* part of her pregnancy. She had something more important to think about than what the catty neighbors might say.

Perhaps a clue is given to us in the words, "She hid herself five months, saying, Thus hath the Lord dealt with me" (Luke 1:24f.). After the parable of the wicked husbandmen, Jesus quoted to the angry Scribes and Pharisees, "This is the Lord's doing, and it is marvellous in our eyes" (Matthew 21:42; cf. Psalm 118:23). He quoted it with the assurance that it was familiar to all His hearers. It was the kind of verse they used themselves. Everyone knew it. This was Elisabeth's refrain during the days she was withdrawn from company. She meditated on the profound mystery of God's gracious dealing with her. She ascribed praise to Him continually.

We can be sure she was concerned more with God's purpose for His people as a whole, than with His goodness to her personally. We can be equally sure she understood that His goodness to her personally was indissolubly linked with His purpose for His people as a whole. Like Mary, she "pondered these things in her heart" (Luke 2:19).

She rejoiced in the message she had read on Zacharias' writing tablet, that the prayers of the nation were answered, that Messiah Himself was about to be born, and that the child of their old age, John, should be His forerunner.

❖   ❖   ❖   ❖   ❖

Mary came upon her suddenly, without warning or announcement. She was an unexpected guest. No arrangement had been made to meet her. "Mary arose in those days, and went into the hill country with haste, into a city of Judah; and entered into the house of Zacharias, and saluted Elisabeth. And it came to pass, when Elisabeth heard the salutation of Mary, the babe leaped in her womb; and Elisabeth was filled with the Holy Ghost: and she spake out with a loud voice" (Luke 1:39ff.).

It was no ordinary sight which moved the elder woman to break out into that Song of Blessing which Luke records. The light of the presence of God shone in Mary's face. She radiated the joy of His hope and the dignity of His service. Elisabeth, who had spent five months in communion with God, recognized a kindred spirit in her relative.

"Elisabeth was filled with the Holy Ghost." This is what she had waited for in the months of her loneliness. The angel had not only assured Zacharias of the impending birth of his son, but he had also promised, "he shall be filled with the Holy Ghost, even from his mother's womb" (Luke 1:15). For this, his wife had "hid herself." She waited for the gift of God which, through her, would reach her unborn son.

When "Elisabeth was filled with the Holy Ghost," she uttered "The Song of Elisabeth." It is perhaps best described as "An Ode to the Virgin."

> *Blessed art thou among women,*
> *And blessed is the fruit of thy womb.*
> *And whence is this to me,*
> *That the mother of my Lord should come unto me?*
> *For behold, when the voice of thy salutation*
> *   came into mine ears,*
> *The babe leaped in my womb for joy.*
> *And blessed is she that believed;*
> *For there shall be a fulfilment of the things*
> *Which have been spoken to her from the Lord.*

The form plainly shows it to be Hebrew poetry. All her life she had loved the Psalms. They had nurtured the springs of her inner life. She knew many of them by heart. In this hour of intense emotion, she instinctively sang in their cadences. Moved by the same Spirit that spake through the Psalmists of old, she entered into the same mood.

The strangest declaration of this Song is not the one in which she elevates Mary as "Blessed . . . among women." It is, rather, the reference to *"the mother of my Lord."*

Yet is it so strange? Three times in his message to Zacharias, the angel used the term "the Lord." "He shall be great in the sight of the Lord." "Many of the children of Israel shall he turn to the Lord." "He shall go before him. . . . to make ready a people prepared for the Lord" (Luke 1:15, 16, 17).

In the privacy of her home, Elisabeth had recited to herself the wonderful and familiar prophecies concerning the Coming One. She had mused on the implications of John going "before him in the spirit and power of Elijah" (Luke 1:17). Like all her co-religionists she was aware of the teaching of the Scribes that the advent of the Messiah must be preceded by the return of Elijah (cf. Mark 9:11ff.).

But Elisabeth had never come to the place where, contrary to everything the Jews believed, she could call another woman "the mother of my Lord."[1] This was spontaneous. To rise to such heights, she needed more than the guidance of the Old Testament. She needed the inspiration of the indwelling Holy Spirit.

If "no man can say that Jesus Christ is Lord, but by the Holy Ghost" (1 Corinthians 12:3), it is equally true that no one could have seen in the simple maid of Nazareth "the mother of the Lord," but by the same Spirit.

*   *   *   *   *

In this short psalm, two different Greek words are translated "blessed."[2] The greeting, "Blessed art thou among women," has reference to God. It means, "Thou art favored of God more than

---

[1] The words used by Luke, ἡ μήτηρ τοῦ κυρίου μου, are in no way related to the theological term θεοτόκος, "Mother of God," which does not appear before the Fourth Century, and certainly has no basis in Holy Scripture.

[2] In Luke 1:42 the verb εὐλογέω is used. Its essential meaning is "to be favored of God," "to be blessed by God." In Luke 1:45 the adjective μακάριος is used. It is a common word which means "happy," "blessed," "blissful."

any other woman." In the subsequent declaration, "Blessed is she that believed," the emphasis is upon the result of God's act. The word "happy" is to be preferred.

From the moment Mary believed God, from the time she accepted her role in God's eternal purpose with the avowal, "Behold the handmaid of the Lord; be it unto me according to thy word" (Luke 1:38), the blessing of God resulted in her happiness.

Although all are endowed with certain inalienable rights, including "the pursuit of happiness," few have learned what Mary knew, that happiness is not an end in itself. It is the result of harmony with the Will of God. "The chief end of man," says the Westminster Catechism, "is to glorify God." When man does that, then, and only then, will he *"enjoy* Him for ever."

The Song of Elisabeth closes on a note of confidence. She is sure that for Mary there will be "a fulfillment of those things which have been spoken to her from the Lord."

The Virgin had had no opportunity of relating her experiences to Elisabeth. We are intended to understand that she was aware of these things because she had received the Holy Ghost.

Elisabeth's assurance was rooted in two things: first, her faith in God; secondly, her own personal experience of God's faithfulness. He who was fulfilling His promise to Zacharias in her would in like manner prove faithful to Mary.

Chapter Sixteen

THE SONG OF MARY

Luke 1:46-55

The glowing words of Elisabeth's greeting needed some reply. No conventional answer would have been adequate.

If Mary was capable of answering the angel in a dignified and humble manner, there is reason to believe she could rise to heights such as this.

This Song is a revelation of the character of the woman who gave to her Son all the share He had in our human nature.

Although replying to Elisabeth, she addresses her first word to God. Mary had a right scale of values.

My soul doth magnify the Lord,
And my spirit hath rejoiced in God my Saviour.
For he hath looked upon the low estate of his handmaiden;
For behold, from henceforth all generations shall call me
   blessed.

This is poetry of a high order. It begins on the level where Elisabeth's ends. It climbs in sublime confidence to greater and more majestic heights. Elisabeth magnifies Mary. Mary magnifies God. Although conscious that future generations will call her "blessed,"[1] she is still the handmaid of the Lord.

She demanded nothing of God. She laid down no conditions. She closed her heart against nothing God might send. She put herself at God's disposal. The literal translation of the word rendered "handmaid" is "slave-girl." She claimed no rights but the right of service.

She recognized that although she was privileged to be the human agent for the accomplishment of God's purpose, all honor and glory must belong to Him. So she praises Him with her whole personality.

[1] It is the word μακάριος again.

> *My* soul *doth magnify the Lord,*
> *And my* spirit *hath rejoiced in God my Saviour.*
> *For he that is mighty hath done to me great things;*
> *And holy is his name.*
> *And his mercy is on them that fear him*
>   *from generation to generation.*

She is very sure that the distinction which is coming to her is due to the God who is not only "mighty" but "holy." The whole psalm is a hymn of praise to the *Mighty* and *Holy* and *Merciful* One. It is probably the happiest song ever sung. God, and God alone, is the Source of her joy.

❋   ❋   ❋   ❋   ❋

> *He hath showed strength with his arm;*
> *He hath scattered the proud in the imagination*
>   *of their heart.*
> *He hath put down princes from their thrones,*
> *And hath exalted them of low degree.*
> *The hungry he hath filled with good things;*
> *And the rich he hath sent empty away.*

Many commentators see in these words a summing up of God's dealings with Israel. Each line, they say, is illustrated many times in the ancient economy.

That, of course, is true. It does not require an extensive knowledge of the Old Testament to call to mind examples of the proud being scattered, princes deposed, the elevation of the lowly, and so on. But such exposition misses the point.

We have here a good example of what linguists call "The Prophetic Perfect." It is the use of the perfect tense to describe a future event. Thus the Prophet sings,

> *Unto us a child* is born,
> *Unto us a son* is given (Isaiah 9:6),

long before the birth takes place. Similarly, "The people that walked in darkness *have seen* a great light" (Isaiah 9:2), does not denote an accomplished fact, but a future blessing. Examples, of course, could be multiplied.

Mary is so sure of God's ultimate triumph in Christ that she is able to state in the past tense the things which will be achieved in the future. She turns away from thoughts about herself. She rises to larger views of God's dealings with men through the coming Messiah. Because it is *all of God,* she can state it as though it were already accomplished.

Mary is not looking back. She is not reviewing God's mercies in the past. She is not concerned with what has already happened. She has the key to the future in her womb. Whatever God may have done with His people in history, she foresees a Gospel which will turn the world upside down.

This strophe is a prophecy of Christ's constant influence on human affairs. It embodies a philosophy of moral achievement which is possible only to those whose spiritual vision is purified by a personal knowledge of a personal God and Father. Spiritual vision does not depend on sight, but on insight. It was Mary's in a high degree.

*   *   *   *   *

> *He hath holpen his servant Israel,*
> *That he might remember mercy*
> *(As he spake unto our fathers)*
> *Toward Abraham and his seed for ever.*

The New English Bible makes this difficult stanza much clearer to our understanding:

> *He has ranged himself at the side of Israel his servant;*
> *firm in his promise to our forefathers,*
> *he has not forgotten to show mercy to Abraham*
> *and his children's children for ever.*

Here Mary returns to the thought of the Age of the Messiah which is about to begin. She sets forth the birth of Jesus as an act of God's grace to Israel. She identifies herself with her people. It is through her that God's promise to Abraham is to be fulfilled. In honoring His promise to her, God is honoring His prior promise to the Patriarch. This is not narrow nationalism. Because the Covenant was made with Israel, it had to be brought to fruition in Israel.

The New Testament nowhere seeks to escape from the doctrine of the "Chosen People." It recognizes that the Jews had mistaken ideas about what this entailed. It condemns them for elevating the idea of privilege, and forgetting the concept of responsibility. It strives to bring them back to the essential element in their relationship with God—that He chose them to be the messengers of His grace and the channels of His purpose.

The birth of Jesus had to take place in Israel. Its significance, however, is to all who fear Him, of all generations, and "of every kindred, and tongue, and people, and nation" (Revelation 5:9), because in Christ "there is neither Greek nor Jew, circumcision nor uncircumcision, Barbarian, Scythian, bond nor free" (Colossians 3:11).

＊   ＊   ＊   ＊   ＊

The *Magnificat*, as the Song of Mary is often called, is not "a hymn of the early Christian Church," composed many years after the event with which it is concerned. It is a source of surprise to me that otherwise sane and scholarly people should argue that such was its origin. There is no external evidence to support such a theory.

The internal evidence is all against it. Is it reasonable to suppose that an Apostle, or an Evangelist, who had lived through the desperate hours of the Crucifixion, and had known the rapturous glories of the Resurrection, would have been silent on such things? Is it reasonable that an accurate reporter, recording the information he had obtained from just such Apostles and Evangelists, would have been mute on these subjects? There are so many places in the *Magnificat* which would have been enhanced by such references.

Neither is the Song of Mary an old Jewish Psalm. True, almost every line can be matched somewhere in the Hebrew Scriptures. But the same might be said, indeed, it often has been said, about a great deal of the teaching of Jesus.

David never praises God in such exalted strains. Even the latest Psalms do not approach the *Magnificat* in insight and devotion.

The Old Testament Songs of Praise lack the sense of *immediacy* which is, perhaps, the central emotion of this lovely canticle. Mary is on the threshold. Her hand is on the latch. It is a moment of transition—the most momentous transition the world has ever known.

Chapter Seventeen

THE SONG OF ZACHARIAS

Luke 1:68-79

This is commonly called the *Benedictus,* from the first word in the Latin translation. It follows the Song of Mary not only in time, and not only in Luke's arrangement of the gospel which bears his name, but also in its sequence of thought.

It is an amazing fact that the first three Nativity Psalms, and, indeed, the first three "Hymns of the Church," all originated in an unnamed city of Judea, in the same house, and in the same room.

> *Blessed be the Lord, the God of Israel;*
> *For he hath visited and redeemed his people,*
> *And hath raised up a horn of salvation for us*
> *In the house of his servant David*
> *(As he spake by the mouth of his holy prophets*
> *which have been since the world began).*

Although the birth of Jesus is still in the future, Zacharias, using the prophetic perfect, speaks of it as if it were an accomplished fact.

While retaining the form and language of the Old Testament, Zacharias breathes the spirit of the New. His emphasis is upon "Redemption" and "Salvation."

The metaphor of the "horn" is common in the Old Testament. "In thy favor our horn shall be exalted" (Psalm 89:17). "The horn of Moab is cut off" (Jeremiah 48:25). "Lift not up the horn" (Psalm 75:4). In such passages the meaning is the same as in Luke. The "horn" symbolizes power. Its exaltation signifies victory and deliverance. To "lift up the horn" denotes independence and pride.

Zacharias here anticipates the great word of the Apostle to the

Gentiles, "The gospel . . . is the power of God unto salvation" (Romans 1:16).

This is not something novel or new. It is not an afterthought on God's part. It is the fulfillment of a promise which is both ancient and oft-repeated. God has never left Himself without witness, and in every age, from the very beginning (cf. Matthew 25:34, John 17:24, Ephesians 1:4, 1 Peter 1:20, Revelation 13:8, 17:8, etc.), "his eternal purpose" (Ephesians 3:11) has been set forth by His messengers, the "holy prophets."

      ✻   ✻   ✻   ✻   ✻

> *That we should be saved from our enemies,*
> *And from the hand of all that hate us;*
> *To perform the mercy promised to our fathers,*
> *And to remember his holy covenant;*
> *The oath which he sware unto Abraham our father,*
> *To grant unto us that we being delivered out of the*
> *   hand of our enemies*
> *Should serve him without fear,*
> *In holiness and righteousness before him all our days.*

This is the purpose of the coming of the Son of the Most High. The Saviour whose birth the inspired priest proclaims is no mere national deliverer, driving back the despised eagles of Rome, and rebuilding the throne of His father David in Jerusalem. Originally, no doubt, "the enemies" from which the prophets foretold deliverance were literal foes (Deuteronomy 33:29, Isaiah 14:2, etc.). But Zacharias was not a man of war. He uses old words, but gives them a new content.

His emphasis, as we have seen, is upon "Redemption" and "Salvation." He interprets these words in the light of the altar rather than of the camp fire. From his long association with the Temple, from his ceaseless study of the sacred scrolls of his people, Zacharias knows the highest, purest and truest meaning of "redemption." He knows the price which has to be paid. He knows that "without the shedding of blood there is no remission of sins" (Hebrews 9:22; cf. Leviticus 17:11).

The salvation of which he speaks is not simply a deliverance from our political enemies who hate us. It is infinitely more than that. It is deliverance from the worst enemy of all—the power of indwelling sin. It is only by such deliverance that we can "serve him without fear, in holiness and righteousness."

The conjunction of "holiness" and "righteousness" implies a double point of view. Zacharias is a priest, but he does not make the common priestly mistake of spelling "right" *"rite."* He sees that "right" is a well-rounded, all-inclusive state. "Holiness" means to be right with God. "Righteousness" means to be right with man. The Christian ideal is the combination of both. John tells us that the proof of our "holiness" is found in our "righteousness" (1 John 2:9, 3:14, 17, 4:11).

*   *   *   *   *

In the closing words of his Song, Zacharias foretells the future ministry of his infant son. He claims fulfillment of the prophecies regarding the forerunner of the Messiah (Isaiah 40:3, Malachi 3:1). He has all the natural pride of a happy father in his newborn son. Yet he does not fail to attribute everything to God.

> *And thou, child, shall be called the prophet of the Highest:*
> *For thou shalt go before the face of the Lord to prepare*
>   *his ways;*
> *To give knowledge of salvation unto his people*
> *In the remission of their sins,*
> *Through the tender mercy of our God,*
> *Whereby the dayspring from on high hath visited us,*
> *To give light to them that sit in darkness and in the*
>   *shadow of death,*
> *To guide our feet into the way of peace.*

It is a beautiful stanza. It reveals a delicacy of spirit, a depth of insight, a richness of faith, and a sensitivity to high and holy things which come only to those who live close to their Maker.

The angel had commanded, "Thou shalt call his name John" (Luke 1:13). Zacharias pondered long over its meaning—"the grace of God," or "the mercy of God." He could hardly help reflecting that his own name, Zacharias, means "remembered by the Lord," while Elisabeth means "the oath of God." He puts them all together. "The *tender mercy* of our God. . . . to *remember* his holy covenant. . . . the *oath* which he sware unto Abraham our father. . . ." Such *paronomasiae*, or plays on words, are quite common in the Bible.

Chapter Eighteen

THE SONG OF SIMEON

Luke 2:29-32

Though Roman troops and unscrupulous taxgatherers caused many folk in Palestine to despair, there were those who waited patiently for the deliverance they were sure God would accomplish.

"They that wait for me shall not be ashamed" (Isaiah 49:23). "I have waited for thy salvation, O Lord" (Genesis 49:18), was the testimony of Jacob. Joseph of Arimathea was also described as one who "waited for the kingdom of God" (Mark 15:43). Devout Jews prayed every day for the advent of the Messiah, using the common petition, "May I see the consolation of Israel."

Among their number was an old and saintly man called Simeon (Luke 2:25). The name is a transliteration into Greek, and then into English, of an ancient Hebrew name. It is first encountered as the name of the second son of Jacob and Leah (Genesis 29:33). This man was the father of "the tribe of Simeon." In New Testament days its commonest form was Simon.

In Luke's description of Simeon, he endows him with higher gifts and qualities than anyone else he mentions in the Nativity Story. Simeon is like Joseph and Zacharias in that he is "righteous and devout" (Luke 2:25). But his excellence does not stop there. He is very much more than that. He is pictured as a man possessed by the Holy Spirit to a remarkable degree.

Luke was not content to say Simeon was a good man full of the Holy Ghost, and leave it at that. He had to specify the Holy Ghost by name three times in as many verses. He says, "The Holy Ghost was upon him" (Luke 2:25). He uses the imperfect tense. This denotes an action begun but not yet ended. The Holy Ghost was *constantly* upon him. In the next verse Luke says, "It was revealed unto him by the Holy Ghost that he should not see death, before he had seen the Lord's Christ." The Spirit of God revealed things to him. The third thing Luke says is, "He came by the Spirit into the temple." He had the practical guidance of the Holy Spirit.

This just and devout man had, therefore, the *inspiration, revelation,* and *direction* of God's Spirit in full measure, and that in the dark hour which preceded the coming of Christ.

❊   ❊   ❊   ❊   ❊

Simeon was an old man. We do not know how old. As we listen to his Song, we are reminded of the lovely thought, "At evening time it shall be light" (Zechariah 14:7). He was so old that he looked forward eagerly to the time of his departure. He had fought a good fight. He longed to finish his course.

It is probable that he remembered the capture of Jerusalem by Pompey, in 63 B.C. This arrogant pagan tore down the veil of the Temple and flexed his muscles in the Holy of Holies. That awful day of mass slaughter was the end of Jewish independence. Simeon had lived through all the shame which followed. He had seen the Temple robbed by the Roman Crassus in 54 B.C. He remembered that fearful time three years later, when Cassius sold thirty thousand Jews into slavery to pay his debts.

Purged by these trials as though as by fire, Simeon looked to God's promise as the only source of personal comfort, and the only hope of Israel. He kept the faith. He sang through the storm. When the Messiah appeared, he was among the few who recognized Him.

The day Mary and Joseph brought the Child to the Temple, old Simeon was praying expectantly, as was his custom (Luke 2:25). As soon as he saw the Babe in His mother's arms, he knew the promise was fulfilled.

Because he himself held the Child, the early Greek Church called him *Theodokos,* which means "the receiver of God." He was singled out for high honor because of this great privilege.

When Mary presented the Babe to him, he immediately began to praise God. Although the Song is popularly known as the *Nunc Dimittis,* the rubric correctly calls it "The Song of Simeon." This rapturous psalm rang through the courtyard filled with soft mauve shadows, when Mary and Joseph moved through the golden half-light "to present him to the Lord; and to offer a sacrifice according to that which is said in the law" (Luke 2:22, 24). The Spirit of God was there to meet the Son of God in His humble entrance into the House of God.

To Simeon's prophetic gaze, the infant Jesus is revealed as the promised Redeemer, for whose advent he had waited so long. Standing in the Court of the Gentiles, he sees in Him a Saviour not only for Jewry, but for humanity.

The vision of Simeon was wider than that of Zacharias, as that in turn was wider and clearer than the vision of Mary. He had lived for many years with his windows open towards the East, waiting for "the consolation of Israel." This was an expression used by the Rabbis to indicate the times of the Messiah.

*　　*　　*　　*　　*

The Song is in three couplets.

> *Now thou art letting thy servant depart, O Lord,*
> *According to thy word, in peace.*

The translation of the King James Version is in error. Simeon does not make a request, but a statement. His heart overflows with thanksgiving that at long last his vigil has been rewarded, and the time has come for him to leave his post. The word of God to Abraham, "Thou shalt go to thy fathers in peace; thou shalt be buried in a good old age" (Genesis 15:15), might be transferred to Simeon.

> *For mine eyes have seen thy salvation,*
> *Which thou hast prepared before the face of all people.*

Here is the reason for his gratitude. Here is the source of his peace at the prospect of death.

Yet all he has seen is a helpless Baby! There has been neither earthquake nor fire. There has been no shaking of the nations. No fearful voice has thundered from the Holy Place. All around him there are religious people going about their affairs in a normal manner. Where, then, is this "Salvation"? God has done nothing.

The Babe *is* Salvation. God has done everything. He has sent His Son, "and in none other is there salvation: for neither is there any other name under heaven, that is given among men, wherein we must be saved" (Acts 4:12). Jesus *is* Salvation. He does not give salvation. He gives *Himself*. It is only as we receive *Him* that we have "the power to become sons of God" (John 1:12).

> *A light to lighten the Gentiles,*
> *And the glory of thy people Israel.*

Jew though he is, he puts the Gentiles first when he comes to sing of the ministry of this Salvation which he holds in his arms. With rare insight, he sees what the Holy Spirit had great difficulty in teaching the early Church a generation, and even two generations, later. Yet it had been clearly indicated in older prophecy: "The Lord hath made known his salvation: his righteousness hath he openly showed in the sight of the nations. He hath remembered his mercy and his faithfulness toward the house of Israel: All the ends of the earth have seen the salvation of our God" (Psalm 98:2f.). "[I will] give thee for a covenant of the people, for a light of the Gentiles" (Isaiah 42:6). "I will also give thee for a light to the Gentiles, that thou mayest be my salvation unto the end of the earth" (Isaiah 49:6).

Yet he uncovers the pride of his old Hebrew heart for all to see. The brief outburst of his psalmody, which begins with a personal strain, and swells out to become universal, ends on a note of rejoicing in "the glory of thy people Israel." There is, however, nothing narrow or selfish, or even nationalistic, in this statement. It is not Messiah bringing glory to His people, so much as His people bringing glory to Messiah. Wiser than his day, Simeon understands that the true glory of Israel must be in the service it renders all mankind in the Name that is above every name.

No one stressed the Jewish element in the opening chapters of Luke more than Renan. Yet he could write of the *Magnificat,* the *Gloria in Excelsis,* the *Benedictus,* and the *Nunc Dimittis,* "Never were sweeter songs invented to put to sleep the sorrows of poor humanity."

The use of the *Nunc Dimittis* in Christian liturgy has been traced to as early as the fifth century. Whether it ever circulated in the primitive Church as a hymn, after the fashion of the *Magnificat* and the *Benedictus,* is difficult to determine.

The Song of Simeon has been placed in many different settings in the Order of Worship. Perhaps John Knox—of all people! —understood it best when he made it the grand climax to his Communion Service.

Part Four

Chapter Nineteen

THE SHEPHERDS

And there were in the same country
shepherds abiding in the field,
keeping watch over their flock by night (Luke 2:8).

The residence of the Shepherds is not mentioned. We do not know where they were keeping watch. We have assumed that Bethlehem is the answer in each case.

There is today, about a mile east of the convent at Bethlehem, a small bedraggled hamlet called "The Village of the Shepherds." Queen Helena built a church in a field there, in the belief that it was the actual field of the Shepherds. The phrase "Let us now go *even* unto Bethlehem" (Luke 2:15), suggests they were some distance away. The Evangelist says they were "in the same country" (Luke 2:8), which merely means "within walking distance." It was customary to keep flocks close to the village during the winter months. They were taken to their distant summer pastures in March, and returned home in November.

Shepherds lived with their sheep. They were a dedicated people. Their life was a hard one. They were exposed to the elements at all seasons. They were denied the simplest amenities of life. They were despised because they always smelled like sheep.

The equipment of the shepherd was standard and simple. He wore a cloak made of sheepskin with the wool left on it. This protected him from the rain and the cold. At night he wrapped himself in it. He made sure his head was covered, even if his feet were exposed. The cloak had an inside pocket large enough to hold an injured or newborn lamb. A bigger sheep needing help was carried "on his shoulder" (Luke 15:5). The shepherd's belt was worn outside the cloak.

Attached to this belt was a wallet. This was a large leather pouch. In it he carried his supplies of coarse bread, sour cheese, raisins, figs, and the small black olives of Judea. It also held the smooth stones he shot from his sling.

The shepherd had a gourd or jar containing his supply of water or sour milk. His staff had no crook. It was a straight pole, about six feet long, slender at one end and a little thicker at the other. He carried a "rod." We would call it a "club." It was a piece of hard, heavy wood, about eighteen inches long, with one end shaped to fit comfortably in the palm of his hand. It was a formidable weapon.

Every shepherd had a sling. It was commonly made of woven goat's hair, though occasionally leather was used. It was a deadly apparatus, used with fantastic accuracy.

There was often a musician among a band of shepherds. He carried a set of reed pipes he had whittled himself. In the brief lilac twilight which suffused the air after their simple evening meal, he would entertain his comrades with traditional airs improvised to suit the occasion.

It was the practice of shepherds to divide the night into "watches," as seamen do. They took turns "standing watch." Their business was to protect their flocks. Sometimes marauders or wanderers would try to steal some of the sheep. More frequently they were attacked by wild animals. If one of these ravenous beasts succeeded in killing a sheep, it was pursued. If possible, it was destroyed, and the portion of the sheep that was left was recovered (Amos 3:12).

It was during one of these "watches" that "the angel of the Lord came upon them, and the glory of the Lord shone round about them" (Luke 2:9) with a brightness so intense the lustrous Syrian stars grew dim as the sky became a burning amethyst. Everything had a patina of light such as the Shepherds had never seen before. "And they were sore afraid." Their lambent eyes popped out. The first word of the angel had to be "Fear not!"

It is no wonder that the prelude to the proclamation was a clear call to abandon fear for, as one of the New Testament writers puts it, Jesus was born to deliver those who through fear were all their lifetime subject to bondage (Hebrews 2:15).

"The angel of the Lord came upon *them*." "The glory of the Lord shone round about *them*." The angel said to *them*, "I bring *you* good tidings." Not Herod. Not Caesar. Not the High Priest. But *Shepherds*—men who were excommunicated by the official religion of the land because of their calling. To *them*—men who were "untouchables." The Lord's messenger appeared to *them*, just as Jesus Himself appeared to the ex-harlot Mary Magdalene after His Resurrection. What kind of witnesses would they make? (cf. 1 Corinthians 1:26ff.).

Suddenly the herald angel was joined by "a multitude of the heavenly host" (Luke 2:13). Their celestial music filled the crisp air. Sublime words demand sublime music for their expression. The words were fixed in the minds of the Shepherds, and found a place not only in the sacred record, but also in the heart of the world.

❖   ❖   ❖   ❖   ❖

A shepherd's life and character have always been a type of simplicity. We have now come to understand that simplicity need not exclude profundity.

Often the shepherd folk, alone with the high mountains and the wide spaces, have peered into unfathomable depths of thought, of which the hurrying, sophisticated world had no time to dream. As compared with the speciousness of courts, the complexity of large communities, and the entanglements of great possessions, the shepherd's life is a simple life, and the shepherd's character is a simple character.

Ever since that unforgettable night when Mary brought forth her first-born Son and laid Him in a manger, many types of devotion have encompassed the marvelous event with their love and praise.

The philosophers and the theologians have come. They have found in the mystery of the Holy Birth a theme for lifelong study and for the exercise of all their wisest faculties.

The kings and the men of wealth have come, bringing more tangible and material offerings, temples of marble, altars of alabaster, and all the pomp of ritual, until the Babe has almost been hidden by the splendors of the devotion that has surrounded Him.

The Arts have come, Painting, Music and Sculpture. They have laid at the feet of the newborn Child the fairest beauty the world could produce, a tribute which was His by right.

Yet the first feet which found their way to Bethlehem were the feet of simple Shepherds. They were poor men with nothing in their hands to bring. They were unlearned men with no powers of complex thinking. They were plain men with no official raiment to trail behind them.

If we could get back into their mood of mind, if we could attain their quality of heart, we might see the glory more clearly than we do. If the simple Shepherds could tell us their secret, it might be to us a gospel and a revelation.

These men were of David's line. They knew the promises of old. They could neither read nor write, but around their fire by night they sang the Psalms of the Shepherd King, and recited the lore of their race which they knew by heart.

The Jews were as full of stories as a pomegranate is full of seeds. The stories were national stories. They were religious epics. They were centered in God's dealings with His people.

We must number the Shepherds among those simple, devout souls who were "looking for the consolation of Israel" (Luke 2:25). Not everyone hears God's proclamation. Now, as then, to millions of people, the birth of Christ means nothing. As Jesus passed from the Cradle to the Cross, it was the few and not the many who caught the Divine ring in His voice. It was not the rich or the influential, it was not the wise or the strong who saw in Him their Hope.

Those who recognized Jesus were people who admitted their need, and wanted to have that need met. There was Nicodemus, the Pharisee, dissatisfied with his own religious experience. There was Zacchaeus, the publican, disturbed about the ethics of his business. There was Mary Magdalene, who had lost her self-respect and longed so desperately to know again the sweetness of life. There was the Roman Centurion, ordered to guard a dying criminal, who saw in His eyes the triumph of his God and Saviour. These were the kind of people who recognized the time of their visitation.

God still speaks to those who hunger and thirst for Him.

> *Think not thou canst sigh a sigh,*
> *And thy Maker is not by;*
> *Think not thou canst wear a tear,*
> *And thy Maker is not near.*
> —George MacDonald

There are many sighs and many tears in our world, but we know, because of what we see in Bethlehem, that God comes to those who look for Him.

The Shepherds were looking for the consolation of Israel.

That is why they said one to another, "Let us now go even unto Bethlehem, and see this thing which is come to pass, which the Lord hath made known unto us" (Luke 2:15).

This statement carries with it an urgency which might be paraphrased, "Let us dash straight across to Bethlehem." They did not care if they went the hard way, so long as it was the quickest way. They were in a hurry.

As you see them hastening off to David's City, they seem to be filled with a boldness which makes them the pioneers of a new courage. A New Testament writer defines it for us: it is "boldness to draw near" (Hebrews 10:19ff.).

It is not a courage lacking in reverence. Its very simplicity is its shield and guide. These men are childlike. Children, although you would not send them out to fight an army, have a boldness which is all their own. They will ask questions and make suggestions which more sophisticated souls would hesitate to express. They will be at home with God in a way which alarms the sinner with his sins, and confounds the sceptic with his doubts.

This is the spirit of those men who "came with haste, and found Mary and Joseph, and the babe lying in a manger" (Luke 2:16). They are bold to draw near. Their simplicity makes them bold. If they need any other boldness, there is martial music still sounding in their hearts, and that is encouragement enough.

We sing,

> *O come, all ye faithful, joyful and triumphant,*
> *Come ye, O come ye, to Bethlehem,*

but it is only the bold, "the faithful," who make this journey. Many of those who seek the road to Christmas will miss the Shepherds' path to Bethlehem.

Plenty of people will find themselves with weary shoppers' feet, and with no redeeming sense of the happiness of giving to gladden and brighten lives in the spirit of Jesus Christ, who was God's own Gift to us.

Plenty of people will be busy with extravagant and elaborate decorations of the home, casting an eye from time to time upon the homes of their neighbors, to see how they are doing in comparison. They will be so busy, they will forget the significance of the light in the window, and the bright decorations festooning the rooms. They will forget that these things are supposed to extend a welcome to the Christ Child on His birthday.

They will take the popular road to Christmas. They will miss the Shepherds' steep track to Bethlehem.

The Shepherds were too excited to follow the road. They climbed over the rough hill, finding their staffs mighty handy. "And they came with haste." Because of this, they found what they sought.

Because Jesus was born in a cave, there was no one to keep them out. It was open for all. There was not even a door.

The contrast between the glory of the heavenly host and the meanness of the stable cannot be exaggerated. When they inhaled the fetid air of the polluted den, these sons of the great outdoors must have wondered, "Do angels come to speak of such things?"

They were as nervous as they were bold. They were still not quite sure what it was all about. They were self-conscious, awkward and stammering. They did not know how to act.

Clive Sanson has vividly recaptured their bewilderment as they stumbled into the tiny circle of illumination thrown by the flickering rushes set in a chink of the wall,

> *There was a star, lady,*
> *Shone in the night.*
> *Larger than Venus it was,*
> *And bright, so bright,—*
>
> *O, a voice from the sky, lady,*
> *It seemed to us then,*
> *Telling of God being born*
> *In the world of men.*
>
> *And so we have come, lady,*
> *Our day's work done:*
> *Our love, our hopes, ourselves,*
> *We give to your Son.*

They learned, simple as they were, that all life was of a piece, shot through and through with the astonishing goodness of God. This assured them that God's goodness included *them*. "The supreme happiness of life," said Victor Hugo, "is the conviction that we are loved." It was this knowledge which came to the simple Shepherds.

They saw that because God's love included them, it included everyone. "And when they had seen it, they made known abroad the saying which was told them concerning this child" (Luke 2:17). The angel had informed them it was for "all people." The circumstances convinced them none would be excluded.

Vision always tends to communicate itself, but the experience is not transferable. Religion is caught, not taught. People catch the love of God from us. However capable the Gospel may be of formal statement, its truest expression lies not in creed but in personal life.

Even the simple Shepherds were "wise men"! They made no secret pact to keep their joy to themselves. They saw it would meet the needs of others too, so they tried their best to share it.

Then "the shepherds returned." The translucent dawn brought them down to earth again. Their sheep needed them. They had commitments. They had responsibilities. They went back to work. There was no trace of pride because of the honor done to them. They had been the earthly heralds of the King of kings, yet they were content to be Shepherds still.

The road back is the hard road. Anticipation, Vision and Realization were behind them. Yet there was no letdown, for they possessed a simple Joy. These men were the pioneers of a new gladness which dawned that winter morning upon a waiting earth. "The shepherds returned, glorifying and praising God for all the things that they had heard and seen" (Luke 2:20).

It was an overflowing gladness. In the rush and power of it these simple shepherds became messengers and apostles. "The first apostles were shepherds, the second fishermen," says Faber.

Whether the witness to Christ be from shepherds, or from fishermen, or from lips more learned and famous, it never rises to the fullness of power unless it has in it something of the gladness of those who have found Christ for themselves, and who, in overflowing gratitude and joy, are eager to share with others the treasure of His love.

Chapter Twenty

ANGELS

> *The angel of the Lord came upon them,*
> *and the glory of the Lord shone round about them,*
> *and they were sore afraid. . . .*
> *And suddenly there was with the angel*
> *a multitude of the heavenly host"* (Luke 2:9, 13).

A distinction is here made between "the angel of the Lord" and the "multitude of the heavenly host."

In the Old Testament, *"the* angel of the Lord" is carefully differentiated from *"an* angel of the Lord." Where the indefinite article is used, it refers to any one of the heavenly beings. Where the definite article occurs, where the reference is to *"the* angel of the Lord," some special messenger is usually indicated.

There are several good examples of this. *"The* angel of the Lord" appeared to Hagar (Genesis 16:7ff.); to Moses at Horeb (Exodus 3:2); to David at the threshing-floor of Araunah (1 Chronicles 21:6ff.); to Balaam (Numbers 22:22); to call Gideon to lead Israel to victory (Judges 6:11ff.); to the mother of Samson (Judges 13:3ff.); to answer Hezekiah's prayer for deliverance from the hand of Sennacherib (2 Kings 19:35); and to Zechariah (1:10ff., see also ch. 2).

Perhaps the references in the book of Zechariah offer the best illustration of this important angel's work. In these verses he appears as the Executive Officer of the heavenly court.

The important thing about the above quotations is that *"the* angel of the Lord" is the same person in each case. He always has the same personality. He seems to be distinct from angels in general. He appears only on important occasions. Indeed, it may almost be said that in the Old Testament he takes the place which is occupied in the New Testament by the Holy Spirit.

On that holy night when he appeared to frightened shepherds in David's fields, to make the announcement for which Israel had long hoped, he was entrusted with the most outstanding task of

123

all. He who had foreshadowed the deliverance of the Children of Israel from the bondage of Egypt here announced the good tiding of great joy "to all people," — the birth of the Saviour of the world.

As soon as he had fulfilled his part, he was joined by "a multitude of the heavenly host." The word "multitude" is not used lightly. We do not know how many there were. Their number must have been considerable. They could not contain their joy. All the benefits were for man, but the angels sang their praises to God.

*   *   *   *   *

Angels are most active in two books of the Bible, the first and the last. It is as if they would claim a share in the entire revelation. In the book of Genesis, one of them brings to Abraham the evangelical promise, "In thy seed shall all the nations of the earth be blessed" (Genesis 22:18). In the book of the Revelation (11:15), others of them give the magnificent fulfillment of that early pledge, "The kingdoms of this world are become the kingdom of our Lord, and of his Christ."

The modern conception of angels as winged—and often feathered—creatures is due to art, not Scripture.

The six-winged *seraphim* are an order of celestial beings mentioned only once in the Bible, in the vision which Isaiah records in the sixth chapter of the book which bears his name. The probability appears to be that this vivid description embodies a symbolism intended to illustrate the tremendous religious truth "our God is a consuming fire"[1] (Deuteronomy 4:24, Hebrews 12:29). "The popular notion of the seraphim as angels is, of course, to be rejected. They are, indeed, more like Titans than placid Gabriels or Raphaels."[2]

The *cherubim* are mentioned more often than the *seraphim*.[3] Yet no one knows exactly what a "cherub" was. The origin and meaning of the word are both in doubt. The Jews regarded them

[1] The word *Seraphim* may come from the same root as the word *Sarrapu,* which was the name of the Babylonian fire-god.

[2] T. K. Cheyne, *Prophecies of Isaiah,* I, 32.

[3] References to *Cherub* and *Cherubim* (plural) are to be found in Exodus 25:19, 37:8f., Numbers 7:89, 2 Samuel 22:11, 1 Kings 6:23ff., 8:7, 2 Chronicles 3:10, Psalm 80:1, 99:1, Ezekiel 9:3, 10:7, 14; 28:14, 16; 41:18. This is a selection of the chief references. It is by no means exhaustive.

as one of the highest grades of angels. In some manner they were associated with "the throne of God," and it is suggested that originally they were believed to be the "throne-bearers." Other traditions, however, make them fulfill the high office of being "the first worshippers," i.e., at the break of day they surround the throne and offer their songs of praise.

It has been suggested that the seraphim were the personification of the lightning, and the cherubim the personification of the thunder—the thunder and the lightning which surround the throne of the Eternal. If so, there might be a veiled reference to them in the familiar words of Psalm 104:3f.

＊　　＊　　＊　　＊　　＊

In the Old Testament, angels are indistinguishable from men. They are "human" in appearance and behavior. Three "men" visited Abraham at his camp near Sodom (Genesis 18). The "men" who helped the family of Lot to escape from the doomed Cities of the Plain were threatened with defilement by the lascivious natives (Genesis 19:5, 15f.). Jacob wrestled with a "man" at Peniel (Genesis 32:24). The Captain of the Lord's Host appeared to Joshua as a "man" with a sword in his hand (Joshua 5:13).

The Old Testament refers to angels under different titles. They are called "messengers" (Genesis 48:16), "sons of God" (Genesis 6:2, 4;), "spirits" (1 Kings 22:19), "holy ones" (Zechariah 14:5), "host of the Lord" (Joshua 5:14), "host of heaven" (1 Kings 22:19), "sons of the mighty" (Psalm 78:25), "watchers" (Daniel 4:14), "host of the height" (Isaiah 24:21), and "God's camp" (Genesis 32:2).

The angels are a medium between the spiritual and the material worlds. Although they are spiritual beings, they are created by God, and dependent upon Him, just as we are. They are abased before God. Unlike the human creation, they are free from bodily infirmities.

In the Old Testament, their functions are to praise God (Psalm 21:29); to carry out His commandments on the earth (Genesis 22:11); to protect the faithful (Psalm 91:11); and to punish the wicked (2 Samuel 24:16f.). Thus, they are God's emissaries. As such, they are divided into "ministering angels," and "destroying angels."

In the New Testament, angels are no longer indistinguishable from men. They are clothed with "the glory of the Lord" when they appear to the Shepherds (Luke 2:9). Their brilliance illuminates the cell in which Peter is confined (Acts 12:7). Although the early visitors to the sepulcher on that first Easter morn are approached by "two men," they are arrayed in such "dazzling apparel" that they are greatly disturbed (Luke 24:4f.).

Paul refers to them in a number of different ways. He calls them "principalities" (Romans 8:38), "powers" (Ephesians 6:12), "thrones" (Colossians 1:16), and "dominions" (Colossians 1:16).

The Old Testament has nothing to say about the "fall" of the angels. The writers of the New Testament twice refer to this (Jude 6, 2 Peter 2:4).

Jesus often spoke of them. He attributed to them a knowledge which, although extensive, was not exhaustive (Matthew 24:36, Mark 13:32). He also pictured them rejoicing over repentant sinners (Luke 15:10).

In the New Testament, their duty is primarily worship (Hebrews 1:6, Revelation 5:11f., Luke 2:13f.). Their function to men is to serve them because men are "heirs of salvation" (Hebrews 1:14).

In the New Testament, as in the Old, their most prominent office is to act as God's *messengers*. The Hebrew word *mal'āk* and the Greek word *angelos* mean "messenger."

Cornelius was informed by an angel that his prayers were heard (Acts 10:3). Peter was delivered from prison by a heavenly messenger (Acts 12:7ff.). During the storm at sea near Crete, an angel appeared to Paul and assured him of ultimate safety (Acts 27:23).

Angels had an important place in the thought of Paul. Three times in his First Epistle to the Corinthians he refers to them specifically. In the first reference (1 Corinthians 4:9), he pictures them watching the affairs of the Church on earth with keen interest. In the second (1 Corinthians 6:3), he says the day will come when the saints judge not only "the world," but even "angels." Probably this remark should be placed alongside other New Testament references to "fallen angels" (cf. 2 Peter 2:4, Jude 6). In his typically Jewish argument for the inferiority of women, Paul says "the woman ought to have authority over her head, because of the angels" (1 Corinthians 11:10). This may well be related to the Old Testament story of the "sons of God" who consorted with "the daughters of men," and produced a race of giants (Genesis 6:2ff.).

There was a tendency in the early Church to worship angels.

Paul had to write very strongly to the Colossians, warning them
against this heresy. He reminded them that Christ has been
given a Name which is above every name, that everything came
into being through Him in the first place, and will be subject to
Him at the consummation of all things. The angels are not
"lesser gods." They are our fellow servants, (Revelation 19:10,
22:9). They must not be worshipped (Colossians 2:18).

❄   ❄   ❄   ❄   ❄

In the Advent story of the appearance of glorious angels to
simple shepherds, there is sounded, for the first time, that note
of harmony between the seen and the unseen worlds which is
expressed again and again in the teaching of Jesus. The angels
who welcomed Him never left Him. As He went about doing
good, He was conscious of them, ascending from Him, and de-
scending to Him.

When Jesus was tempted in the wilderness, far from any human aid, "the angels ministered unto him" (Mark 1:13). In the
terrible ordeal of Gethsemane, when His closest friends slept like
clods, an angel strengthened Him (Luke 22:43). Twelve legions
of angels, more loyal than the twelve disciples who wanted to
sit on twelve thrones judging the twelve tribes of Israel, were
ever at His service (Matthew 26:53). The honor guard at the
Empty Tomb was made up of sentinels from heaven (John
20:12).

Perhaps this explains that delightful yet puzzling word of
Jesus, which suggests that each of us has a guardian angel who
is specially concerned with our own individual welfare (Matthew
18:10).

Angels are all over the place in the Nativity Story. Mary believed them. So did Joseph. And the Shepherds.

To believe the angels, to trust the God of the angels, to adore
the Lord whose heralds they were, is to know more than Mary,
Joseph, or the Shepherds ever knew. For the truth at which the
angels merely hinted deepened in force and beauty as the Child
grew to manhood, "and dwelt among us, and we beheld his
glory, glory as of the only begotten of the Father, full of grace
and truth" (John 1:14).

Chapter Twenty-One

GOOD TIDINGS OF GREAT JOY
TO ALL PEOPLE

It is, perhaps, surprising to discover that the gospel references to "joy" mostly occur either at the very beginning, or at the very end, of the story.

The angel proclaimed "Good tidings of great joy . . . to all people" (Luke 2:10). Mary "rejoiced" (Luke 1:47). Elisabeth's kinfolks came to rejoice with her in the birth of John the Baptist (Luke 1:58). Simeon and Anna were almost beside themselves with joy when Jesus was presented at the Temple (Luke 2:25ff.). The Magi "rejoiced with exceeding great joy" when they saw the Star (Matthew 2:10).

Jesus Himself spoke of joy at the very time we should least expect Him to do so—at the end, when there seemed to be no future and no hope.

It was on that dreadful night in which He was betrayed. He was sharing His last meal with His friends. Suddenly, out of the blue, He began to talk to them about "joy."

The shadow of the Cross had darkened everything that night. Without understanding it, the disciples felt something monstrous was about to happen. Everything was somber and cold. Yet Jesus spoke to them of His "joy"—and of their "joy" too (John 15:11, 16:20, 22, 24, 33).

Later on, the disciples showed they had understood. You have only to read the Acts of the Apostles to feel you are back again in the atmosphere of Christ's own presence. Read it in the light of Paul's testimony, "We were afflicted on every side; without were fightings, within were fears" (2 Corinthians 7:5). That special reference is to Macedonia, it is true, but that happened to be one of the better places!

The early Apostles had a rough time. Of course they saw the dark side of life! They were persecuted, imprisoned, tortured. Of course they were often afraid! They never knew what a day would bring forth. But bravery does not mean the absence of fear. It means the conquest of fear. "Joy" does not mean a perpetually clear and bright sky. It means the sun is always there, even if dark clouds obscure it momentarily. The Apostles conquered their worst fears because they knew that, come what may, God's eternal sovereignty could not be affected.

Their confidence is superbly expressed by Paul in the cherished words, "Who shall separate us from the love of Christ? shall tribulation, or anguish, or persecution, or famine, or nakedness, or peril, or sword? . . . Nay, *in all these things* we are more than conquerors through him that loved us. For I am persuaded, that neither death, nor life, nor angels, nor principalities, nor powers, nor things present, nor things to come, nor height, nor depth, nor any other creature, shall be able to separate us from the love of God, which is in Christ Jesus our Lord" (Romans 8:35ff.).

The road may be rough and steep. The battle may be fierce and long. The adversaries may be numerous and powerful. But at the end of the road there are many mansions. The result of the battle will be victory for God's people. After the opposition of the enemy there is the eternal fellowship of the eternal glory. And at every step of the journey there is the companionship of Almighty God Himself.

The joy of the Christian is not based on self-confidence. Its source — its only source — is the sovereign love of the Holy God. It is, therefore, a religious joy.

* * * * *

That is the joy of Christmas. It is a *religious* joy. It must be. We rejoice *in the coming of God*. We rejoice in the coming of God *in a form we can grasp.*

> *He laid His glory by,*
> *He wrapped Him in our clay.*
> —Charles Wesley

Isn't that sufficient grounds for rejoicing? How can any man realize that God loves him without being deeply stirred in thought and affection?

Apart from the message of Bethlehem, our Christmas festivities have as much life as a pressed flower. As you cannot have light and warmth without the sun, so you cannot have permanent joy unless your life is rooted in God — as He is revealed in Jesus.

This is the theology of the angelic declaration. The message is one of joy because it declares *God's act*. "God hath visited and redeemed his people" (Luke 1:68).

In the gospel according to St. Luke, the "dear and glorious physician" sets forth the facts of Christ's life and ministry as they were experienced among His own people, the Jews. In the Acts of the Apostles, he continues the story. He shows how the "good tidings of great joy" were carried from Jerusalem to "Judea and Samaria, and unto the uttermost part of the earth" (Acts 1:8), in a word, "to all people."

In the second treatise we can follow the Gospel as it spreads from the Upper Room in Jerusalem to temples, houses, streets, market places, ships, countries, cities, islands, and districts everywhere.

We can follow it as it is received by Jews, Scythians, Romans, Greeks, Ethiopians, Egyptians, barbarians, magistrates, centurions, soldiers, scholars, eunuchs, prisoners, freemen, women, children, slaves, fugitives, and honored matrons.

It is "good tidings of great joy to all people," and to all people it has come. Its message is, "There is born to you this day in the city of David a Saviour, which is Christ the Lord" (Luke 2:11). "Hallelujah! The Lord God Omnipotent reigneth."

Chapter Twenty-Two

THE SIGN

When the angel of the Lord appeared to the Shepherds, clothed in "the glory of the Lord," "they were sore afraid" (Luke 2:9). But as the King's herald proclaimed Messiah's birth, they forgot their fears. They were caught up into the seventh heaven. All the prayers of Jewry were being answered at this time. The announcement was made to them.

They believed the angel. They did not ask for a sign. They were "out of this world" in ecstasy. The angel gave them a sign unasked. He gave them the sign to bring them "down to earth" once more.

I do not think it is necessary to enter fully into a discussion of the complex problems which are inevitably associated with the giving of signs. However, some things need to be said.

At His Temptation (Matthew 4:1ff., Mark 1:12f., Luke 4:1ff.), Jesus spurned the suggestion that He should obtain a following in the same way a magician seduces the credulous. He wasn't going to pull any fancy stunts like jumping off the Temple roof. Why?

Well, for one thing, what about those who were not there to see it? What would they say to Him when He visited their town? (cf. Luke 4:23).

One of the many penetrating observations in that greatest of all religious plays, *Green Pastures*, is put into the mouth of God, "When you pass a miracle, the worst of it is that you have to rear back and pass another—and you never really get any further."

We ought to remember that every time Jesus was asked for a sign He refused to give it. He had nothing good to say about people who wanted signs (Matthew 12:38f., Mark 8:12f., Luke 11:29ff., John 4:48, 6:30).

In this respect we should recall the visit of the disciples of John the Baptist to Jesus. It is one of those incidents which is

131

beset with difficulties. It is hard to reconcile the object of the
visit with two other New Testament facts. The first is the statement that John was in some way related to Jesus (Luke 1:36).
The second is that John proclaimed Jesus to be the Promised
One, either at His Baptism, or elsewhere (Matthew 3:11ff., John
1:29ff.). Yet we are told that John sent his disciples to ask Jesus
the question, "Art thou he that should come, or do we look for
another?" (Matthew 11:3).

Jesus refused to give them a straight "Yes" or "No." He told
them to go back to their master and tell him the kind of things
He was doing.

This is not a case of a foolish question receiving a foolish
answer. It is, rather, an excellent example of a foolish question
receiving a sound answer. The question was stupid because the
evidence was there all the time, making it unnecessary.

The same applied to the business of signs. The people who
asked for them were blind to the spiritual evidence which was
all around them. If they could look upon all the good Jesus did
and still ask for a supernatural vindication of His authority, they
were more than foolish people asking foolish questions. They
were people who had no right to ask the question at all, for they
showed themselves to be totally insensitive to spiritual values.
If they were not convinced by *Jesus Himself* — by the presence
of the Son of God among them — what would it take to convince
them?

We ought to make a distinction between "signs on earth" and
"signs from heaven." Jesus gives us plenty of earthly signs.
Everything He did, every word He spoke, was a sign of what
He was.

He sums up His philosophy of signs in that remarkable con-
versation with Nicodemus, "If I have told you earthly things,
and ye believe not, how shall ye believe, if I tell you of heavenly
things?" (John 3:12). To this we might add the conclusion of
the parable of Dives and Lazarus, with its dreadful finality, "If
they hear not Moses and the prophets, neither will they be persuaded, though one rose from the dead" (Luke 16:31).

Most important of all, we must realize that there are signs
and signs. The ugliest, vilest, and most vicious thing this world
has ever seen — the Cross — is the incomparable sign of the most
beautiful, the purest, and the most gracious thing possible — the
redeeming holy love of God.

The whole subject of "signs" needs re-examining. Perhaps

Jesus is saying to those who crave signs today, "Get thee behind me, Satan: thou art an offence unto me: for thou savourest not the things that be of God, but those that be of men" (Matthew 16:23).

*   *   *   *   *

The angel said to the Shepherds, "This is the sign unto you: Ye shall find a babe wrapped in swaddling clothes, and lying in a manger" (Luke 2:12). That probably shook them more than anything else.

Had they heard correctly? Surely the least they could expect for the sign of such an event would be an outstanding miracle. It would be a sign at least comparable to the rod of Moses turning into a serpent (Exodus 4:2ff.), or the sundial of Ahaz being reversed to convince King Hezekiah that God would heal him (2 Kings 20:8ff.). Yet they were not even granted the miracle of a star hovering over "where the young child was" (Matthew 2:9).

The problem was not that the sign was commonplace. It was worse than that. Babies were common enough, but who, except the outcast or the poverty-stricken, would put a baby in a manger? That was a place for cattle fodder. "A babe . . . lying in a manger."

But for the forewarning of the angel, this was the only child in Bethlehem they would have passed by without a second glance. The manger would have been an insurmountable stumbling block to them.

They were looking for a "Saviour." The angel had spoken of "Christ" — the Anointed of God for the redemption of the world. He had used of Him a title which really belonged to Almighty God Himself — the *Lord*. Who would look for "the Lord's Anointed" in a manger?

Yet this was *the* sign. They would recognize Him, not in spite of, but because of, His low estate. They would find Him, of whom all the prophets had spoken, in a *manger*.

It is difficult to grasp such condescension. It is also hard to imagine a bigger difference between what the Shepherds expected and what they received. Yet, as Wordsworth so finely remarked, "Wisdom is oft-times nearer when we stoop than when we soar."

Christmas and Easter have more in common than we generally realize. It is Paul who speaks of Christ's Crucifixion as "a stumbling block" (1 Corinthians 1:23). He also refers to "the offence of the cross" (Galatians 5:11). The hideous death of Jesus was not the kind of thing the Jews expected of the Messiah. Neither was His birth.

"*The* sign," the *only* sign, was enough to deflate the hopes of the Shepherds immediately. "Ye shall find the Saviour ye seek, who is Christ the Lord, in the form of a helpless babe." It was utterly incongruous. "*Lying in a manger.*" Could that be possible?

The Birth, the Ministry and the Death are all of a piece. If Jesus could not get a hearing by talking or by works — not of power for power's sake, but of mercy for love's sake — He would do so by dying.

This is still the religion, not perhaps for the wise and the prudent, if indeed there really are any such, but for the "babes" (Matthew 11:25; cf. 1 Corinthians 1:18ff.), which the vast majority of us still are.

"God was in Christ," not browbeating the world, but "reconciling the world," the world, not as it ought to be, but as it is, "unto himself" (2 Corinthians 5:19).

The Sign of the Cross and the Sign of the Manger are valid indications of how God works. Not "how God *worked*," but "how God *works*," for He is still active in our world today *in just the same way*. It is thus that God works in the laboratory, in art, music, and literature, and in the daily life of ordinary men and women. His presence is disguised rather than advertised.

It is Bethlehem all over again. If His birth is heralded by a heavenly song, it is heard only by those whose very simplicity permits them to perceive what is plainly obvious. If the Star in the East is seen by the Wise Men, it is because, as well as being wise, they are searching the star-strewn skies, and are aware of the world's need of a Saviour.

As Son of God, our Lord will live unknown and unrecognized by the great and the clever. The obscurity of His birth is but a premonition of the circumstances of His earthly ministry, and a perfect prelude to a perfect life of perfect service.

When God entered human life in His Son Jesus, He did not "suddenly appear in his temple" to overawe us. He stooped down, "and dwelt among us."

> *I come in the little things,*
> *Saith the Lord:*
> *My starry wings*

I do forsake,
Love's highway of humility to take:
Meekly I fit my stature to your need.
                    —Evelyn Underhill

The Shepherds did not go to Bethlehem seeking the birth of a great man, or a famous teacher, or a national hero. They were promised a *Saviour*.

The manner of His Birth indicates the character of His Salvation. God seeks to establish with us "a gracious personal relationship" in which our personalities, rather than being violated, are brought to their true fulfillment. "Meekly I fit my stature to your need."

There was a miracle, of course. It was the greatest miracle of all. The fact that it was veiled in a manger made it all the greater. "The Word became flesh, and dwelt among us" (John 1:14).

As we look at the Babe on His bed of straw, we are reminded that we must become dependent as little children, if we would enter the Kingdom of God.

Chapter Twenty-Three

PEACE ON EARTH

The two most famous hymns in the Bible are contained in single verses. In the sublime vision of Isaiah, the seraphim chant,

> *Holy, holy, holy, is the Lord of hosts:*
> *The whole earth is full of his glory.*
> (Isaiah 6:6)

In Luke's account of the first Christmas, "a multitude of the heavenly host" sings,

> *Glory to God in the highest,*
> *And on earth peace among men*
> *with whom he is well pleased.*
> (Luke 2:14)

The Angels' Song consists of two obvious divisions. In each of these there are three parts which, true to the structure of Hebrew poetry, parallel each other exactly. The three parts of the first line are "Glory," "God," "in the highest." They correspond respectively with "Peace," "men with whom he is well pleased," and "on earth."

The Song of the Angels is known as the *Gloria in Excelsis.* Its occasion is the birth of the Messiah. The words are not prophetic. They are exclamatory. There is no suggestion that these things *shall be.* It is confidently asserted that *they are.* Here we are not dealing with wishful thinking, or hopeful prayers. We accept, or we reject, a majestic affirmation. We shall return to this.

"Glory" is one of those great words which you almost have to *feel.* It defies adequate definition. Yet we must define and illustrate it as best we can.

The root meaning of glory is *worthiness.* However, we use the word in two senses. When we speak of "the glory of God" we mean His unutterable splendor. We imply that He is supremely and uniquely *worthy* because He is the sum of all perfection. When we talk about "giving glory to God," we use the word in the sense of "adoration," "worship."

In the New Testament, many facets of God's *worthiness* are revealed in the various *glorias* offered to Him. The Samaritan who had been healed of his leprosy returned "to give glory to God" for the marvelous benefit he had received (Luke 17:18). Because Abraham's faith in God's promise did not waver, he gave "glory to God" (Romans 4:20). Herod Agrippa usurped the majesty due to God alone. He was slain because "he gave not God the glory" (Acts 12:23).

When the Elders worshipped God, saying, "Worthy art thou, our Lord and our God, to receive the glory and the honor and the power: for thou didst create all things, and because of thy will they were, and were created" (Revelation 4:11), they set forth the creatorship of God as valid grounds for giving Him the glory. They were acknowledging that everything has its origin in God and depends upon God. Because of this, everything should confess His glory. In the great fifth chapter of the Revelation, glory is ascribed to "him that sitteth upon the throne, and unto the Lamb" for the redemption they have wrought.

    ❊   ❊   ❊   ❊   ❊

The Angels glorify God because of the Peace which became incarnate in the Babe of Bethlehem.

The Jews believed their coming Messiah would be "The Prince of Peace" (Isaiah 9:6). As such, He would establish "peace on earth." This was a *motif* of Hebrew prophecy. It resounds in their great songs.

> *In his days shall the righteous flourish;*
> *And abundance of peace, till the moon be no more*
>   —Psalm 72:7

> *They shall beat their swords into plowshares,*
> *And their spears into pruning-hooks;*
> *Nation shall not lift up sword against nation,*
> *Neither shall they learn war any more.*
>   —Isaiah 2:4

It is interesting and enlightening, as well as surprising, that the Hebrews were the first people in the world to cherish peace. They were the only people desiring peace when Jesus was born. In spite of the *Pax Romana* which the able Augustus had established, war was not outlawed. It was not repudiated as a means to an end. The lull was at best temporary.

The ancient world — with the exception of the Jews — regarded war as a noble occupation. It looked to the field of battle for the exercise of man's highest virtues. It regarded war as natural. The question whether war was right or wrong had not arisen. The imperfect moral standards of the time saw nothing objectionable in war. Indeed, if we may draw a modern parallel, the Apache braves of the nineteenth century would have been very happy in the first century. It spoke their language.

It was into such a world that the message of the first Christmas came, "Peace on earth, among men with whom he is well pleased."

It was revolutionary. It reversed the popular idea of God Himself. It contradicted all the Romans and Greeks had ever believed about their gods. It exposed the errors of the Jews in those early days when their devotion was directed to a tribal deity. It demanded a new appraisal of theology itself.

The message which came that first Christmas was, "Peace on earth *among men with whom he is well pleased."* We have no right to lift "Peace on earth" out of the context. God is "well pleased" with those who give Him the glory. He is "well pleased" with those who see His hand in the passing events of time. He is "well pleased" with those whose chief aim in life is to serve and please Him. He is "well pleased" with those who put first things first. That means He is "well pleased" with those who put Him first in all things. To them He sends His gift of peace. The gift is never divorced from the Giver. To have peace, you must have the Prince of Peace.

The Angels do not proclaim any peace but the peace of God. When we give God His rights, He guarantees ours. We can know "the peace of God" only when we have "peace with God, through our Lord Jesus Christ" (Romans 5:1). "He is our peace" (Ephesians 2:14). That is why the New Testament speaks of "the God of peace" (Romans 15:33, 2 Corinthians 13:11, 1 Thessalonians 5:23, etc.), as well as "the peace of God" (Philippians 4:7, Colossians 3:15, etc.).

When the Angels sang of "Peace on earth," it was not a hazy and indefinite human relationship they meant, but the living presence of the "Prince of Peace," whose birth the herald-angel had just announced.

The essential thing about the glad Christmas season is not what happens outwardly, but what we experience inwardly. There cannot be "peace on earth" — in the sense of freedom from war, fear, oppression, and exploitation — until there is "peace among men." There will never be "peace among men" until they are "men with whom he is well pleased." It was failure to understand the *inwardness* of this which caused the poet to write,

> *Strange Prophecy! if all the screams*
> *Of all the men that since have died*
> *To realize war's kingly dreams*
> *Had risen at once in one vast tide,*
> *The choral song of that vast multitude*
> *Had been o'erpowered and lost amid the uproar rude.*
> —S. T. Coleridge

We must not confuse the message of the Angels with the get-well-quick advertisements from Madison Avenue. There is no fast-FAST-F A S T solution of this problem.

The angelic declaration is not a magic formula, guaranteed by Good Housekeeping. Neither is it pledged to rid the earth of all its troubles in a few seconds, or double your money back.

The Angels do not offer a do-it-yourself gimmick for those who are handy with the tools of self-improvement. Peace is not the achievement of man. It is the gift of God.

Total peace is the harmony between our nature and our environment. Our truest environment is spiritual. "In him we live, and move, and have our being" (Acts 17:28). The great reconciling Word of the Incarnation is that Jesus came to lift us into harmony with Himself. He became one *of* us that we might become one *with* Him. This is something we cannot do for ourselves. It is all of grace (Ephesians 2:9). This alone can create the inner harmony of spirit by which we are at peace with ourselves, and so prepared to be "at peace with all men" (Romans 12:18).
The object of the Gospel is not to create barriers, but to break them down.

You can warm yourself in the glow of the Christmas story. You can share in the vague goodwill which is in circulation for a brief time at this season of the year. But the only real warmth comes from being close to the fires of the Divine love. *Goodwill is in constant danger of crumbling, unless it is reinforced by the presence of the indwelling Prince of Peace.*

In the manner of His coming, we see the Word of God for every generation. It is not enough to know that God became Man. We must know what kind of man He became.

It is not enough to know that Christ was born at Bethlehem, or even to understand that at Christmas we celebrate the Holy Birth. We ourselves must take the road to Bethlehem. We must find there, for ourselves, the answers to our personal questions. We shall find the answers embodied not in a philosophy, but in a Babe.

There was once a German ruler who wished to possess a Cremona violin. He offered an unheard-of price. It was published in every market place throughout the realm. For months he had no success.

Then one day an old man appeared at the castle gate. He was poorly dressed. He had a shabby violin case under his arm. The servants refused to admit him.

Finally, "because of his importunity," they agreed to carry his message to their master. He asked them to say, "Heaven's music is waiting at your door."

The Prince ordered him to be admitted immediately. The old man drew from the worn case a perfect violin. He soon created marvelous music which won the Prince's ardent praise.

"The violin must be mine. Name your own price," said the Prince. The old man shook his head. "I want no money," he said; "the violin may be yours only on condition that I pass my life within your house, and use the instrument every day." The Prince accepted the violin on these terms.

❖   ❖   ❖   ❖   ❖

In the last week of His life, Jesus saw the gleaming Temple crowded with worshippers. They were all beseeching God for peace. There were tears on His cheeks because the people of God did not know God when they saw Him. "If thou hadst known. . . . the time of thy visitation" (Luke 19:42, 44).

God speaks to man when he is silenced by the pressure of his burdens, when he is brought low by a sense of his own impotence. He spoke to Elijah when he was on the verge of suicide, and to Job when he was reduced to beggary.

God speaks to us in these dreadful days. He speaks now, when barbarous cruelty and utter lack of morality corrupt and degrade the affairs of whole nations; when the slave-cars of Russia are again transporting their hapless victims to the wilds of Siberia; when the bearded fanatics of Cuba, forgetting God, are, perhaps, causing the rest of the world to remember Him.

God speaks to us, now, because our need is so great. But how much attention do we pay to Him? How sensitive are we to His voice?

If Jesus were born in Bethlehem of Judea *this* Christmas, and the information reached the great wire services, this is what we should hear over our radios and television:

"We interrupt our program to inform you that we have just received a bulletin of an event the consequences of which will change the whole course of human history. But first, a word from our sponsor!"

The Master Musician waits outside our door. He offers us the harmonies He alone can create. He, as the "Prince of Peace," can make us "men with whom he is well pleased."

Let us recall the lovely Prayer of St. Francis:

Lord, make me an instrument of Thy peace.
Where there is hatred, let me sow love;
Where there is injury, pardon;
Where there is discord, union;
Where there is doubt, faith;
Where there is despair, hope;
Where there is darkness, light;
Where there is sadness, joy.
O Divine Master, grant that I may not so much seek
To be consoled, as to console;
To be understood, as to understand;
To be loved, as to love;
For it is in giving that we receive;
It is in pardoning that we are pardoned;
It is in dying that we are born to eternal life.

Part Five

Chapter Twenty-Four

THE WISE MEN

> *Three Kings came riding from far away,*
> *Melchior and Caspar and Balthasar;*
> *Three Wise Men out of the East were they,*
> *And they travelled by night and they slept by day,*
> *For their guide was a beautiful, wonderful star.*
> —H. W. Longfellow

The nationality of the Wise Men is not disclosed. It is simply stated that they came "from the East" (Matthew 2:1). To the Jews, Assyria was the "north," and Babylon was the "east."

Babylonian astrologer-priests had studied the stars for more than three thousand years. They had defined and named the main constellations. They had introduced the twelvefold division of the Zodiac. The Babylonians gave Abraham to the Jews. The father of the faithful came from Ur of the Chaldees (Genesis 11:31). It was a land of portents, a strange and compelling land. It would be fitting if the Wise Men were Babylonians.

It was early believed they came from Persia. Persia, beyond Babylon, was known as "the far east." There, astrologers built high towers, which were the world's first "observatories." From them they charted the courses of the heavenly bodies. They connected these movements with events on the earth, especially with important births.

In the old Median language, *mog,* or *mag,* meant *priest.* The Medes were divided into six tribes, one of which was the *Magi,* corresponding to the Levites among the Hebrews, the Druids among the Celts, and the Brahmins among the Hindus.

Matthew's word for "Wise Men" is *Magi.* At first it was a title of honor. The Wise Men were credited with great wisdom in philosophy. They were thought to possess rare skills in natural science and medicine. They were held in very high repute. Later on, the word lost its nobler meaning. Among the Greeks and Romans it was the general designation of all who claimed supernatural knowledge of any kind. Gradually it came to be used only of charlatans and dabblers in the black arts. It has come down to us in the word "magician."

History has immortalized Matthew's Wise Men as earnest seekers after truth, willing to follow the light of a star in the belief that it would bring them to the light of God.

Most likely the Magi were pious men, whose minds had ascended from nature to nature's God. They had noted that the Supreme Being was not dealing with them, or with others, as they deserved. He was dealing with them in mercy. This whetted their appetite for more knowledge of Him. They pursued their studies to this end.

Being students of lights, they are represented as longing to bow themselves in adoration before "the true light which lighteth every man that cometh into the world" (John 1:9).

When they saw the Star, they immediately associated it with the birth of "the King of the Jews" (Matthew 2:2). This suggests they, too, were "waiting for the consolation of Israel" (Luke 2:25).

They may have searched the Old Testament Scriptures, and become acquainted with the prophecy of Balaam, "There shall come a star out of Jacob" (Numbers 24:17). The book of Daniel was very widely read among the Gentiles, and the Wise Men may have learned of Israel's Hope from that source. Wherever they came from, there were many Jews in the land where they lived. Some of them were noted for their scholarship. They were to be found in most schools. The Wise Men may have learned of the coming One from them. It may have been revealed to them directly by Almighty God Himself.

However the knowledge came to them, the important thing is *they acted upon it.*

No doubt many people said the Wise Men were foolish to venture on such a journey. They would have to cross many a weary desert. They would have to climb many a rugged mountain pass. They would have to ford many a swirling river. They would be exposed to the scorching sun by day. They would shiver in the cold winds of the night. They would be in danger from wild beasts and robbers, from floods and droughts, from sickness and exhaustion.

The Wise Men had a strong sense of purpose.

As they came from the East
Following a star,

One said
The sun burns,
The moon changes,
Stars are faithful.

One said
They shine in all tongues,
Every heart knows them,
By starlight there are no borders.

One said
The world widens
By starlight,
The mind reaches;
Stars beget journeys.
—John Erskine

Among a nation of materialists, they were men who believed in spiritual values. They craved to know the mysteries of fuller, deeper life. They had seen a Star. Obey it they must.

They came, these priestly astrologers, across the Euphrates and the Tigris, over the wind-swept desert, till their laden caravans approached Palestine. Enchanted, they watched the amethyst colors deepening on the far mountains of Samaria and Moab. They listened to the larks rising and falling on their fountain of song in the last glow of sunset.

They anointed themselves with spikenard and attar of roses as became their station in life. Their keen eastern faces were bronzed by desert suns. Their short beards were virile, and glistened with the perfumed oils of Araby. From under thick black brows their Orient eyes gleamed like polished steel. Their noses were the noses of eagles, beaked, and more than a little wild. Their full red lips were masterful, and could be very cruel.

They represented the scientists of their age. They observed a new star, and their "science" led them to Jesus. It was not the Star which led them. It was the inferences they drew from what they observed.

They had a strange religion. It was full of queer superstitions. Yet they were groping after God, if haply they might find Him. God led them by the light they had to the birthplace of Jesus. "God," said St. Chrysostom, "caught the Magi with a Star!"

Matthew tells us (2:2, 9f.), that the Star which they saw when they were in the East was not visible to them during their journey, so that, for the greater part of their way to the Holy Land, they had to "walk by faith, not by sight." It first appeared to announce Messiah's birth. It was His Natal Star. When it reappeared at Jerusalem, they were filled with "exceeding great joy" (Matthew 2:9f.).

They were looking for a King.

Kings are usually born in king's palaces. It was natural for them to inquire in the city where the king lived. It was inevitable, after that, that they should be brought into the presence of Herod. They had known him by name and reputation for many years. They had heard stories of his magnificence they could hardly credit, and reports of his building schemes they had dismissed as exaggerations. A dark crimson was drifting through the fronds of the palms as they followed their guides through courtyards and terraces gleaming with alabaster and gold. The scent of jasmin rose in clouds in the warm air.

To their amazement, they found themselves confronted by a shrewd businessman. He was interested in their story. He was concerned for their comfort. He was suave and convincing. He put on none of the airs they had expected him to show. He talked to them intelligently, as a man of affairs. He knew the customs of their country. He asked solicitously of people they discovered to be common friends. When they were at their ease, he suggested he might be in a position to help them.

He summoned "the chief priests and scribes of the people" (Matthew 2:4). It was not a formal gathering of the Sanhedrin. Herod merely called together those who could furnish the required information. When he asked them where the Christ should be born, they answered mechanically, without interest or concern, "In Bethlehem of Judea: for thus it is written by the prophet, And thou Bethlehem, in the land of Judah, art not least among the princes of Judah: for out of thee shall come a governor, that shall rule my people Israel" (Matthew 2:5f.). Then they went back to their daily round and common task.

It is an incredible picture. The chief priests and scribes of the people knew every jot and tittle of the ancient prophecies.

Yet when they had answered the question addressed to them, they lost all interest. They were Philistines. A Philistine, you remember, knows the price of everything, and the value of nothing. There is not the slightest suggestion that these "teachers of Israel" thought it worth while to invesigate for themselves whether something was happening at Bethlehem. They returned to their accustomed routine.

The Wise Men from the distant East left all to follow the Star. They had only to mention their mission to the crafty, worldly-wise old king, for him, from entirely different motives, to appreciate its importance. But the men it should have concerned the most were disturbed the least.

It was entirely fitting that the man of affairs and the truth-seekers should turn to the men of religion in their perplexity. It was natural that these custodians of the Law should be able to supply an answer from their accumulated knowledge. It was dreadfully wrong that these sages should leave it to half-informed foreigners to verify their information, while they did nothing about it.

They prayed daily for the coming of God's Elect. They claimed to be earnest people, who believed in God, and wanted above all else to live by His Law.

What they really wanted was not a Saviour who would convict them of sin, redeem them from sin, and admit them into the life of glory. What they really wanted was a king who, by his might, would substantiate what they already were, undergird the kind of life they already had, support and sustain them in their pride, and confirm them in their sense of their own righteousness.

This has been the curse of God's people from the earliest time until today — this sense of self-righteousness; this pride; this inability to admit in the presence of God that they are wrong, and in the presence of man that they do not know everything.

According to Matthew, it was in the very hour of the Nativity that the religious leaders of the Chosen People missed the greatest opportunity of their lives, and showed themselves to be "blind leaders of the blind."

When the chief priests and scribes of the people departed, Herod sent the Wise Men to Bethlehem with his "blessing." He asked them to return with the information he desired (Matthew 2:7f.).

"When they had heard the king, they departed; and, lo, the star, which they saw in the east, went before them, till it came and stood over where the young child was. When they saw the star, they rejoiced with exceeding great joy. And when they were come into the house, they saw the young child with Mary his mother, and fell down, and worshipped him: and when they had opened their treasures, they presented unto him gifts; gold, and frankincense, and myrrh. And being warned of God in a dream that they should not return to Herod, they departed into their own country another way" (Matthew 2:9ff.).

It is wrong to suggest that the Wise Men broke their promise to Herod when "they departed into their own country another way," because there is no evidence that they had made such a promise.

*   *   *   *   *

It seems to be one of the most firmly established facts of life that we are led into new fields of knowledge, wider realms of experience, and a deeper world of understanding, by seeking the pot of gold at the rainbow's end.

Our development, our wealth of being, indeed everything about us, is bound up with this business of following the gleam. Scientific research has often had a background which was no more substantial than a dream, a will-o'-the-wisp, an intuition, an idea. The unreal led to the real. The imaginary led to the actual. Illusion gave place to knowledge. Fact followed fiction. The rainbow's end may not have been where they hoped to find it. The important thing is that they did find it. And there was the pot of gold, in the shape of a "breakthrough."

These priest-scientists of the East discovered the end of the rainbow. It was in Bethlehem, not Jerusalem. It was in a humble dwelling, not a king's palace. But their quest was successful. Their dreams were realized. Their hopes were fulfilled.

Then, for their own sakes, as well as for the sake of the Babe, "they departed into their own country another way." They had made their plans well. They had a detailed knowledge of the geography involved. They had alternate routes they could follow if it became necessary. Their thoroughness paid off. As suddenly as they appeared, they disappeared.

Chapter Twenty-Five

MICAH

When the Wise Men came to Jerusalem enquiring, "Where is he that is born king of the Jews?", they revived the terror which had never been long absent from the mind of Herod.

He had never known the feeling of security. He had never been so safe on his throne that he could relax his vigilance. Sometimes greedy men try to overthrow haughty tyrants in order that they may themselves become haughty tyrants. It is so today. It was so in the days of Herod the King. He had to be constantly on guard. He might be King of the Jews by the favor of Caesar, but he remained King only because he possessed the military might to beat off any challenger.

This new threat came from a source veiled in obscurity to the Edomite. He immediately summoned the nation's leaders to resolve a question any ten-year-old Jewish child could have answered.

"When he had gathered all the chief priests and scribes of the people together, he demanded of them where the Christ should be born. And they said unto him, In Bethlehem of Judea: for thus it is written by the prophet, And thou, Bethlehem, in the land of Judah, art not least among the princes of Judah: for out of thee shall come forth a governor which shall be shepherd of my people Israel" (Matthew 2:4ff.). This is a free rendering, rather than an exact quotation, of Micah 5:2. When we remember that most of the references to the Old Testament were from memory, the marvel is that they were so good.

❈   ❈   ❈   ❈   ❈

It is most fitting that the prophet Micah should be introduced in the Advent story. Not only was he the first to focus the hopes of Israel upon a personal Redeemer, but his idea of religion is closer to the New Testament than anything else we find in the Old.

Micah came from the small southern village of Moresheth (Micah 1:1, Jeremiah 26:18). Assyria's *blitzkrieg* was gathering momentum. He recognized the inevitability of impending doom. Like Amos (Amos 7:7ff., 8:2f.), he saw in Assyria the agent by whom the iniquity of the country was to be punished. He prophesied that Assyria would despoil not only the Northern Kingdom of Samaria (1:6), but also the Southern Kingdom of Judah (1:10ff.). He foretold the destruction of Jerusalem (3:12) a full century before Jeremiah.

Micah was more concerned with the lot of the underprivileged and dispossessed farm laborers than the wealthy landlords in their fine town houses. The widow's cottage meant more to him than the magnificent Temple. This has led some people to think that Micah himself was the victim of oppression, that the family farm on which he grew up in Moresheth had been seized for debt by avaricious money-lenders (cf. 2:2f.).

At any rate, the words of Isaiah which Jesus quoted at the very beginning of His public ministry, "The Spirit of the Lord is upon me, because he hath anointed me to preach the gospel to the poor; he hath sent me to heal the brokenhearted, to preach deliverance to the captives, and recovering of sight to the blind, to set at liberty them that are bruised" (Luke 4:18; Isaiah 61:1), contain both the spirit and the fervor of Micah.

A degenerate aristocracy (2:1ff., 7ff.), a "supreme court" composed of corrupt judges (3:1ff., 9ff., 7:3), a mercenary priesthood (3:11), and the venal prophets who spoke fair words to those who paid them (2:11, 3:5f.), must be wiped out, not because Micah desired it, but because the righteousness of God demanded it (6:1ff.).

The book of Micah has been described as uniting the pessimism of Amos with the Messianic optimism of Zechariah. Its fervent evangelical faith was evidently dear to the heart of our Lord, for He seems to have referred to it, or quoted from it, with affection and facility.

Micah's picture of national disaster is not the end of the story. It is followed by a vision of restoration. The hope of this revival, however, does not lie among the priestly caste in Jerusalem. It is not to be found in the capital city at all. It will come from one of the most insignificant of Jewish villages, Bethlehem. "But thou, Bethlehem Ephratah, though thou be little among the thousands of Judah, yet out of thee shall he come forth unto me that is to be ruler in Israel" (Micah 5:2).

Bethlehem was the home of David (1 Samuel 16:4, 17:15). It was so closely associated with him as to be almost identified. If the mention of "David" did not provoke the reaction "Bethlehem," the mention of "Bethlehem" certainly brought to mind the name "David."

However, when Micah says the Deliverer shall emerge from Bethlehem, he does not indicate merely the stock from which the root shall spring, but its character, its nature. Like David, He will be "one of the people."

You have only to read the story of David, as it is contained in the books of Samuel, to discover that a deep cleavage existed between the royal court and the common people. Saul's jealousy was based on the fact that David really was the popular idol. He was the hero of the common people because he was one of themselves. Saul the son of Kish had become haughty, proud, autocratic and remote.

When the Evangelist says of Jesus, "The common people heard him gladly" (Mark 12:37), we need not be surprised. He was one of themselves. He not only spoke in a language the masses could understand, He also spoke as one of them. Like Micah, He, too, was one of the peasants from the country. Like Micah, He drew pictures which were familiar to His hearers.

Micah promised a Governor who would restore the simplicity and openness, the fairness and justice, which the Hebrew patriot always associated with the son of Jesse. When Jesus was born, Mary "laid him in a manger, because there was no room for them in the inn." That may contain a parable of our Lord's relationship to the society of His day.

❋   ❋   ❋   ❋   ❋

Micah joined with the other eighth-century prophets, Amos and Hosea in the Northern Kingdom, and Isaiah, his great contemporary in Judah, in a desperate effort to purify the religion of the time. Micah is often close to Amos. Like him, he displays a deep moral earnestness which does not shrink from drawing the ultimate conclusions (Micah 3:12, Amos 2:5, 5:1f., etc.). Like Isaiah, he reveals a profound insight into the nature of God. It was this which determined his concept of religion (Micah 6:6ff., Isaiah 57:15; etc.). Like Hosea, though not to the same extent, he had begun to believe in "grace." He speaks tenderly of God's care and affection for Israel, in spite of the waywardness of the people (Micah 4:6f., 6:3f., 7:18ff., Hosea 1:7, 2:19, 6:6, 11:1ff., etc.).

The national religion had come to be regarded as a kind of celestial insurance policy. So long as the people paid the premiums, in the form of sacrifices and ceremonies, through the accredited agents, the priests, they considered themselves safe (Micah 3:11). Morality and right-dealing were forgotten. Rite was more important than right.

The same situation existed when Jesus was born. John the Baptist denounced it, "Think not to say within yourselves, We have Abraham to our father: for I say unto you, that God is able of these stones to raise up children unto Abraham" (Matthew 3:9). They took no more notice of John than they had of Micah.

They persisted in the same attitude towards Jesus. "They answered and said unto him, Our father is Abraham. Jesus saith unto them, If ye were Abraham's children, ye would do the works of Abraham" (John 8:39).

This is the emphasis of Micah. He gave the world its noblest definition of religion, "He hath shewed thee, O man, what is good; and what doth the Lord require of thee, but to do justly, and to love mercy, and to walk humbly with thy God" (Micah 6:8).

He also drew one of the loveliest pictures in the Bible of what it will be like when that concept of religion is put into practice. "The mountain of the Lord's house shall be established in the top of the mountains, and it shall be exalted above the hills; and people shall flow unto it. And many nations shall come, and say, Come, and let us go up to the mountain of the Lord, and to the house of the God of Jacob; and he will teach us his ways, and we will walk in his paths: for the law shall go forth out of Zion, and the word of the Lord from Jerusalem. And he shall judge among many people, and rebuke strong nations afar off; and they shall beat their swords into plowshares, and their spears into pruninghooks: nation shall not lift up sword against nation, neither shall they learn war any more. But they shall sit every man under his vine and under his fig tree; and none shall make them afraid: for the mouth of the Lord of hosts hath spoken it" (Micah 4:1ff.).

Chapter Twenty-Six

"WE HAVE SEEN HIS STAR"
Matthew 2:2

> Star Light, Ingle Light,
> Light of the countless years!
> This night is Thy Night,
> Monarch without compeers.
> Dark was the world at Thy coming,
> Life a terror and gloom;
> But now men's hearts go homing
> To an Inn that could find Thee no room;
> An Inn with a stable and manger,
> In a little Syrian town,
> And a tiny meek-eyed Stranger
> That lured the bright angels down.
> —Lewis H. Court

The Bible has a great deal to say about stars. At creation, they were set "for signs, and for seasons, and for days and years" (Genesis 1:14). Scripture repeatedly forbids the worship of the stars (Deuteronomy 4:19, 17:2f., 2 Kings 21:2f., Amos 5:26, etc.).

The Psalmist regards them as the noblest work of the Creator (Psalm 8:3, 19:1). Both the Old Testament and the New Testament writers refer to the vastness of their number (Genesis 15:5, 22:17, 26:4, Exodus 32:13, Deuteronomy 10:22, 28:26, Jeremiah 32:22, Nehemiah 9:23, Hebrews 11:12, etc.).

There have been three main theories regarding the Star of Bethlehem.

It has been dismissed as a myth, the creation of pious imagination. This has been the attitude of those who deny the possibility of miracles.

Some scholars who allow the possibility of the miraculous, but seek to keep miracles to a minimum, have argued that this Star was a natural phenomenon. It was a real star. It was an ordinary star. It may have been a new star. It may have been a conjunction of planets. Whatever it was, it occurred in the natural order of things.

In A.D. 1614, the noted astronomer Johann Kepler calculated that a conjunction of Jupiter and Saturn took place in 7 B.C. In a similar conjunction that he personally observed in 1604 A.D., a particularly bright star appeared between the two and then gradually faded away. It has been argued that such a star may have been the one to arouse the interest of the Magi.

The third view, and the only one which fits all the reported facts, is that the Star that appeared in the heavens to awaken the curiosity of the Wise Men, and start them on their costly and perilous journey to Jerusalem, was a Divine creation specially suited for the purpose.

Sixteen hundred years ago that great Church Father, St. John Chrysostom, advocated this view as the only correct interpretation of the Biblical story. He pointed out that the Star appeared in broad daylight; that it could be seen even though the sun was shining; that it came and went at will; that it had no fixed course, but preceded the Wise Men from Jerusalem until it hovered over the place where Jesus lay. No ordinary star behaves in such a manner.

It is no more strange that there should be signs in the heavens at the Advent of the Messiah than that there should be angelic proclamations and songs. No more strange, indeed, than that a pseudo-messiah should subsequently call himself Bar-Cochba, "Son of a Star."

Whatever the Star of Bethlehem was, Christ the Lord was born, and herald angels sang. The deeps of the sky were opened. Men were told that the Saviour of the world was born. They were assured that His Kingdom should have no end.

❋   ❋   ❋   ❋   ❋

Legend and fancy have not neglected the Star. According to Eastern tradition, this was such a miraculous planet that those who saw it could clearly distinguish the Virgin and the haloed Child in its center! Another ancient story said it showed a young child bearing a cross! But the one which really goes the whole hog is the phantasy of Gregory of Tours, who maintained that the heavenly body was really an angel, which somehow fell into a well at Bethlehem, where, in his day, (A.D. 538-594), it could still be plainly seen!

Perhaps in our thinking about Christmas we emphasize the Star too much. The real issue is not astronomical fact. It is the lofty business of the soul. The Star is the symbol of guidance and, in this case, what it meant is of far more importance than what it was.

All our problems are made easier if we have some guidance on them. If there is no such thing as guidance, not only does the entire Christian religion fall to pieces but life itself loses its meaning and purpose.

"All I ask is a tall ship and a star to steer her by." The ancient mariners in their sailing vessels knew the value of the stars. Sometimes they were caught in a storm, or in the darkness. If they could see their star, they were not alarmed. They could steer in the right direction. They could be sure of the way. Even if they had been buffetted and driven off their course, they could still get back on it, for their star was fixed and constant.

The significant thing about a star is that it can be seen most plainly in the darkness. It is in the darkness that our need of assurance and direction is the greatest.

The Wise Men were not searching for a Star. They were seeking a Babe. Astrology, in its scrutiny of the sky, is but a confession of *need*. It is a need which is so great that it can be met only from beyond our earth.

There is in the heart of every man something that makes him long for guidance. This is shown not only in the weird cults that arise from time to time but also in the persistence of palm-readers, fortune-tellers, astrologers, and the like.

We need to know that life means more than existence. We need to know that there is an ultimate goal. We need to know the way to that goal. We need to know that we are not alone.

Christmas brings us the message of "Immanuel." The Star guides us to Him who is "God with us." It shows us the glory of God in the face of Jesus Christ. It gives us the confidence not only that there is a goal to life, but also that He will help us reach it. This is the truth of Christmas that remains when all the festivities are over.

The Star remains sure and constant. By its light we can see the Way, know the Truth, and live the Life. John Calvin used to say, "The heavenly Father chose to appoint the Star and the Magi as our guides, to lead directly to His Son."

It is not enough that we should *see* the Star. The Magi not only saw it, they *followed* it. They were wise because they allowed themselves to be led by it. They were wise because they accepted the guidance it offered.

> *Starlight, Splendour,*
> *Charming the kings of old:*
> *Came they far to render*
> *Frankincense, Myrrh, and Gold;*
> *Over the Araby sand-dunes,*
> *Out of their magic East,*
> *Sages, tired of their hoar runes,*
> *Came to Thine Advent Feast:*
> *Star of a deathless glory,*
> *Star of the World's Hope still,*
> *Light of the Old, Old Story*
> *Bright above Bethlehem hill.*
> —Lewis H. Court

As we have suggested, there were probably others who saw the same Star. They paused for a moment, casually to remark on its brightness. They did not find the Christ-Child. They did not make the supreme discovery of life because they were content to be spectators. They were not willing to become followers. They were not willing to pay the price.

The Star always demands a price. Indeed, it leads us to the words of Jesus, "If any man would come after me, let him deny himself, and take up his cross daily, and follow me" (Luke 9:23).

> *But the Babe was the Hope of the ages,*
> *And the Star of that first Yule-tide*
> *Made stale the lore of the sages,*
> *And a crown for One crucified.*
> *And down the long generations*
> *The Star that shone at His birth*
> *Is challenging still the nations*
> *That long for true peace on earth.*
> *Bring Him the holly berry,*
> *The mistletoe, white as His fame!*
> *For to make us holy and merry*
> *The Christ-Child of Bethlehem came.*
> —Lewis H. Court

Chapter Twenty-Seven

GOLD, FRANKINCENSE AND MYRRH

The Wise Men brought three gifts for the Child. Gold, Frankincense and Myrrh. These were all notable products of the mysterious region loosely called "The East."

We must not, however, forget that while they came with these presents in their hands, the Magi also brought Him the gift of their hearts.

The Wise Men confronted the people of Jerusalem with the startling question, "Where is he that is born King of the Jews?" (Matthew 2:2). Because they were seeking a *King*, they came prepared to pay *tribute*.

The Old Testament speaks of the gifts which the Queen of Sheba brought to King Solomon (1 Kings 10:2, 10f.). When David subdued the Philistines and the Moabites, they acknowledged his suzerainty by bringing gifts (2 Samuel 8:2). The fame of Uzziah, king of Judah, was very widespread. During his reign of fifty-two years, he extended the borders of his kingdom in every direction. "And the Ammonites gave gifts unto Uzziah" (2 Chronicles 26:8).

When Pekah, monarch of the Northern Kingdom, entered into an alliance with Rezin, king of Syria, to attack Judah, and destroy it as an independent realm, Ahaz and his court fell into a panic (Isaiah 7:1f.). They lost their heads so completely they sought aid from their worst enemy, the Assyrian invader. "So Ahaz sent messengers to Tiglath-pileser king of Assyria, saying, I am thy servant and thy son: come up, and save me out of the hand of the king of Syria, and out of the hand of the king of Israel, which rise up against me. And Ahaz took the silver and the gold that was found in the house of the Lord, and in the treasures of the king's house, and sent it for a present to the king of Assyria" (2 Kings 16:7f.).

King Jehoshaphat became extremely wealthy because of the tribute he exacted from neighboring countries. The Philistines

156

paid an annual levy of silver. The Arabs contributed a percentage of their rams and goats. He built fortifications and storehouses with the revenue (2 Chronicles 17:11f.).

To make a gift to a sovereign was to admit, and accept, both his authority and his power. To refuse to make a gift to a king was to deny his authority and challenge his power. Ancient art offers many examples of vanquished peoples standing in line, waiting their turn to pay homage to their conqueror. The Magi were following a well-established precedent. They were seeking a King. It was, therefore, natural and proper to carry gifts.

✿   ✿   ✿   ✿   ✿

Gold has always been a precious metal. It had great purchasing power, not only in the East, but also in the "South" — in Egypt, where soon the Child was to find refuge from the wrath of Herod.

Although the words "gold" and "goldsmith" are found in several books in the Old Testament (e.g., Genesis 2:11, Joshua 7:21, 1 Kings 9:11, Isaiah 40:19, etc.), the Jews never became as expert in the craft as some of their neighbors.

Many of the Temple vessels were of pure gold, while others were of pure silver (1 Chronicles 28:14ff.). They were, of course, of Jewish manufacture. However, the designs were simple and the workmanship often amateurish.

The Egyptians, on the other hand, perfected such exquisite goldwork that, although some of the archaeologists' discoveries are almost five thousand years old, they cannot be matched by the most cunning artificers of today.

Gold has never been mined in Palestine. The chief gold-producing areas of the ancient world were Arabia, Spain and Africa. Arabia included Seba and Ophir, whose gold was regarded by the Hebrews as the finest in the world (Job 28:16, 1 Chronicles 29:4). Some of them would no doubt have preferred the Eldorado of Arabia to "the land flowing with milk and honey"!

If we follow the example of the Wise Men, we shall not worship gold for the things it can buy. We shall give it to the King for His service. We shall not use it "as we please," but as pleases Him. We shall offer Him the tribute due from loyal subjects who rejoice in His reign.

The value of our tribute is not calculated on a cost basis. It is relative to what we have left. In this mid-twentieth century, there are more homeless people in the world than ever before.

At Christmas time we sometimes think unkindly of those who made it so hard for the Holy Family. It would be more profitable to act kindly towards those who, in our day, are in need of hospitality.

*   *   *   *   *

The Magi traveled towards the setting sun to find a God. They came to worship. John Ruskin once said to his class, "These men, for their own part, came — I beg you very seriously again to note this — not to see, not to talk — but to do reverence. They were neither curious nor talkative, but submissive." They came *prepared* to worship. Long before they reached the humble shrine, they had packed gifts of frankincense on their beasts of burden.

Frankincense was used in prehistoric times. Produced in India, it was imported into Palestine through Arabia (Isaiah 60:6, Jeremiah 6:20). It is a kind of gum, or resin. It is obtained much as we obtain maple syrup. An incision is made into the trunk of the tree. The bark is removed to a depth of five inches below this wound. The incision is deepened a few weeks later. The gum exudes in large, clear globules which are scraped off and placed in a specially prepared basket.

Frankincense is mixed with other ingredients to make incense. The word "incense" comes from a Latin term meaning "to burn." It is a mixture of gums and spices. It produces a perfume when burned. The incense employed in the service of the Tabernacle was made of stacte, onycha, galbanum, and pure frankincense. The Jews discovered there were other formulas for making the incense. Any deviations from the above recipe were called "strange," because they were not strictly *kosher*. It was early forbidden to use such products (Exodus 30:9).

Incense was sprinkled on the offerings that were presented to God in the Temple. It disguised the stench of burning flesh. The sweet odor of the incense ascended to God with the chants of the priests and the prayers of the faithful. It spoke of worship and supplication.

Frankincense was used for sacrificial fumigation (Exodus 30:34f.). It is called "frank" because of the freshness with which, when burned, it gives forth its odor. It burns for a long time with a steady flame.

Frankincense could be offered only to God.

The Wise Men offered Jesus the frankincense of their devotion. Their offering was accepted. They found favor with God. Under His providential care, they returned safely to their own land.

It may well be that the frankincense of our devotion stinks in the nostrils of God, because it hides from us the stench of the evils of our age. If we use it as a sanitizer, it is not an offering, it is an insult.

*   *   *   *   *

When Simeon took the Child in his arms in the Temple Court (Luke 2:28f.), he sensed the cruel death He should die. It may be that the Magi, wise beyond their knowing, perceived He was to die for all mankind, the "Saviour, who is Christ the Lord," "born that man no more may die."

At any rate, they brought to Him myrrh. This was more suited for a funeral than a birth. Yet it was not out of place, for the King to whom they brought their gold, and the God who was worthy of their frankincense, was also the Son of Man who was born to die. He was "the Lamb slain from the foundation of the world" (Revelation 13:8).

Myrrh is a gum-resin which exudes as yellowish-brown "tears" from a shrub that is found chiefly in Africa. Because of its extremely bitter taste, it was used to keep moths out of clothes (Psalm 45:8), much as we use cedar chips and moth balls today.

When Jesus was crucified, it was offered to Him as an analgesic (Mark 15:23). Tradition has always made myrrh the symbol of death.

But it was very much more than that. It is listed as the first ingredient of the holy anointing oil (Exodus 30:22). This was used to mark everything connected with the worship of God. When a person, or thing, was anointed, it was "set apart." It was marked as "sacred." The real meaning of "sacred" is "belonging to God."

The word *Messiah* means "The Anointed" in Hebrew. *Christ* means the same thing in Greek (cf. John 1:41). When Peter and John returned to the waiting disciples after being arrested for preaching the Gospel, they said, "The kings of the earth stood up, and the rulers were gathered together against the Lord, and against his Christ [i.e., *Anointed*]. For of a truth against thy holy child Jesus, *whom thou hast anointed*, both Herod and Pontius Pilate, with the Gentiles, and the people of Israel, were gathered together, for to do whatsoever thy hand and thy counsel determined before to be done" (Acts 4:26ff.).

The myrrh was not only a sign of His foreordained death, it was also an indication of His Messianic Office. It was for "the Lord's Anointed." From the beginning of His earthly existence, He was "Sacred," "set apart" as "belonging to God." "When the fulness of the time was come, God sent forth his Son, made of a woman, made under the law, to redeem them that were under the law, that we might receive the adoption of sons" (Galatians 4:4f.).

The offerings we lay on His shrine are not acceptable unless we ourselves have been "set apart" as "belonging to God."

As the Wise Men stooped low over the Child, with their costly gifts in their hands, the Star yet shining bright above, the magic of their divination lay in their knowledge that this Child was God and King and Saviour.

This is still the only knowledge that can make us "wise unto salvation."

> *Christians, lo! the star appeareth;*
> *Lo, 'tis yet Messiah's Day;*
> *Still with tribute treasure laden,*
> *Come the Wise Men on their way.*
>
> *Where a life is spent in service,*
> *Walking where the Master trod,*
> *There is scattered Myrrh most fragrant*
> *For the blessed Christ of God.*
>
> *Whoso bears his brother's burden,*
> *Whoso shares another's woe,*
> *Brings his frankincense to Jesus*
> *With the men of long ago.*
>
> *When we soothe earth's weary children,*
> *Tending best the least of them,*
> *'Tis the Lord Himself we worship,*
> *Bringing gold to Bethlehem.*
>
> *Christians, lo! the star appeareth,*
> *Leading still the ancient way,*
> *Christians, onward with your treasure,*
> *It is still Messiah's Day.*
> —James A. Blaisdell